Teaching Teens About Relationships

Teaching Teens About Relationships

A Guide for Teachers, Counselors, and Youth Group Facilitators

Chuck Rhoades

ROWMAN & LITTLEFIELD
Lanham • Boulder • New York • London

Published by Rowman & Littlefield
An imprint of The Rowman & Littlefield Publishing Group, Inc.
4501 Forbes Boulevard, Suite 200, Lanham, Maryland 20706
www.rowman.com

86-90 Paul Street, London EC2A 4NE, United Kingdom

British Library Cataloguing in Publication Information Available

Library of Congress Cataloging-in-Publication Data

Names: Rhoades, Chuck, author.
Title: Teaching teens about relationships : a guide for teachers, counselors, and youth
    group facilitators / Chuck Rhoades.
Description: Lanham : Rowman & Littlefield, [2024] | Includes bibliographical
    references and index. | Summary: "Teaching Teens About Relationships describes how
    to teach a relationships course for adolescents. This book includes learning activities
    and instructional strategies that give teens access to a safe environment to discuss
    issues that are in the forefront of their lives"—Provided by publisher.
Identifiers: LCCN 2023035481 (print) | LCCN 2023035482 (ebook) | ISBN
    781475873375 (cloth ; alk. paper) | ISBN 9781475873382 (paperback ; alk. paper) |
    ISBN 9781475873399 (epub)
Subjects: LCSH: Interpersonal relations in adolescence.
Classification: LCC BF724.3.I58 R46 2024 (print) | LCC BF724.3.I58 (ebook) | DDC
    158.20835—dc23/eng/20230907
LC record available at https://lccn.loc.gov/2023035481
LC ebook record available at https://lccn.loc.gov/2023035482

Contents

Preface

The idea for a course on Relationships for high school students came while I was teaching a Health course for sophomores at Portsmouth (NH) High School. The one term, 45-session course covered a wide scope of health topics divided into units. With a background in sexuality education and sensing the high level of interest to students, I designed the sexuality unit to be the longest unit, which meant about three weeks. The second longest unit, mental health, took about two weeks, with nutrition/fitness and chemical awareness (substance use) units

While fortunate to work with students who responded to my interactive teaching style in all of the units, it was clear that energy and engagement peaked during the sexuality and mental health units. Like many health instructors, I felt there was never enough time to fully explore the issues we examined, such as gender identity and orientation, decisions about sexual behaviors, communication skills, and psychological stresses, and mental illness. But the most prominent topic, crossing into both the sexuality and mental health units, was clearly relationships. I allotted three or four days in the sexuality unit explicitly to a relationships mini-unit, which included discussions on expectations and responsibilities. Students also collected data from peers and adults on how these participants defined an intimate relationship, desirable qualities in a partner, how relationships start, areas of agreement and disagreement, good ways to end a relationship, and what is important to give and get in a relationship. This treasure of information gave each class much material to discuss and evaluate. Typically, the bell signaling the end of class cut our discussions short.

In the mental health unit, a mini-unit on stress gave students the opportunity to identify stressors in their lives, which we would then fictionalize and use as content for learning stress management skills. Invariably, many examples of stress in their lives came from relationships with family, friends, and partners. In both of these mini-units, students' yearning to go further, deeper, and longer matched my growing frustration at not having the time in the Health course to accommodate their needs.

So, in 2006, I proposed a term-length course to my department chair, the guidance department, and school administration as a Health elective. The Health course was the only prerequisite, which meant that students in grades 10–12 were eligible to enroll. I delighted in its gaining quick approval.

I had many ideas and many resources in designing the initial course offering, which happened in the Fall Semester, 2007. I designed many original activities and adapted many from other professional sources, including some from higher education. During this time, I also taught a Human Sexuality course at the University of New Hampshire and several psychology courses at Hesser College while teaching at the high school. My consultant work experiences with an agency serving homeless and runaway youth also contributed to the course. Discussions with those students gave me invaluable insights into how they would have benefitted from having relationships taught when they were in high school. I included many of their suggestions in my high school course.

Incorporating student perspectives and experiences was essential to the course's success. Students created their own material for use in acquiring and practicing relationship skills. Students provided the content to work with activities addressing communication issues, problem areas, sexual touch, and identification of important relationships in their lives. They provided an extensive and diverse content that formed the basis of our discussions. This student-centered approach gave me access to their experiences, concerns, values, and strengths. The course gave them access to a safe environment to discuss issues that were in the forefront of their lives.

Course development became an on-going process as I became aware of new resources and identified student needs and requests. I constantly experimented and re-worked the instructional design. The teaching experience continually sparked and challenged my creativity and comprehension of adolescent relational development. I taught Relationships until the 2019–2020 school year, when it ended with my pandemic-induced retirement. Some clichés fit. If my students learned from me, I certainly learned as much from them.

Who took the course?

The initial enrollments were sparse. In the first offering, six students sat in the class. The second course had eight. Nearly all were students who had taken my Health course and liked my teaching style. A few took it simply because it fit into their schedule. While understanding that sometimes new courses took time to take hold, it was still discouraging.

Then something clicked. Word of mouth from the students who took the course, guidance counselors making referrals, and my overcoming my reluctance to announce the relationships course to my health course students came into play. Suddenly, there were 12–15, 20, and then 25. I hoped for 10–15, as that felt like the optimum class size and that thankfully was the typical enrollment.

Besides students who knew me from the Health course, LGBTQ+ students frequently registered. Being the faculty advisor to the Gay Straight Alliance for 15 years factored into this draw. Seniors formed the largest class in each course. They took the course as an elective, often in their final semester. Students who participated in theater productions were noticeably represented. There were athletes in every class.

Other than those who simply enrolled for scheduling reasons, students tended to be interested in the course for personal growth and understanding. Most were in relationships at the start of the course. Many of these were not by its end. In retrospect, I think that many of these students may have taken the course to examine their relationships, having some unidentified hesitancy or ambivalence that the course helped them clarify.

Initially, the course enrollment largely consisted of students identifying as female. There was a very uneven gender ratio for a few years. Then, again due to word-of-mouth, more students identifying as male joined the course. Many years had at least one transgender student in the class.

Acknowledgments

My family deserves to be acknowledged first and foremost. My relationships with Melanie, Emily, and Rachel Rhoades are the most important in my life.

I am fortunate to have two daughters-in-law, Mallory Cordes and Mal Ali and four grandchildren: Caleb, Lachlan, Anson, and Breccan. I am grateful that Caleb showed me his special place and that Lachlan found a peanut. The good natures of the twins are a delight.

Members of my extended family fed me with love at various times as I taught the course and during the writing of this publication. Thanks to Mike and Janet Reing, Linda Chambers, Chelsea Valentine, Mary Earnest, Katie Reing and Tom Reing.

There are dear friends whose ongoing support and caring have sustained me over the years personally and professionally. Thanks to Patrick Ganz, Allan Lurvey, Joyce Rizzo, Veronica Roth, Greg Schwartz, and Richard Stoltz.

I have had the good fortune to work with many wonderful colleagues throughout my professional career. Among those I treasure most are those whose generosity of spirit and ideas and whose relationship I value deeply: Kristine Baber, Cathy Bradeen-Knox, Beth Casarjian, Carolyn Cooperman, Joni Foster, Mary Madden, Jody Pierce-Glover, and Mary Ruchinskas.

Thanks to my colleagues at Portsmouth High School for fostering healthy relationships every school day.

This work is dedicated to every student who took the relationships course. May your personal relationships be as fulfilling as your commitment to this course.

Introduction

Since I taught this course in units, this publication is similarly organized. I did not incorporate every activity or even every unit in each section of the course that I taught. I approached each class, as many teachers do, as a unique experience, tailoring content and methodology to the students in a particular class. My choice of these different approaches came from my perception of the groups' dynamics, learning styles, interests and experiences.

Parts of this course were used in work with youth in group counseling sessions and in multi-session programs with youth in group homes and transitional housing. In the body of this work, the terms *youth* and *students* and *class* and *group* are interchangeable.

I usually involved the students in determining content, but there were some core components that I maintained through almost all sections of the course. Consistent methodologies included experiential activities, dyad and small group tasks, music and artistic expressions, role-playing, writing exercises, and quizzes. We spent the most time in large group discussions, where we processed activities or films. The content addressed in every course included beliefs and theories about relationships, mindfulness and communication skills, starting, building, and ending relationships, sexual experiences, problem-solving, and defining love.

Each course gave youth the opportunity to define relationship issues and problems they were interested in examining. The most frequent choices they made involved sexual decision-making, infidelity, jealousy, outside influences on romantic relationships, and resolving conflicts.

The first chapter describes how to start the course. As a group-building process, each session builds on the previous one. The sequence is important to maintain. The second chapter explains instructional practices that I used throughout the course. Each subsequent chapter comprises a unit and the approximate sequence of sessions that I used. Each course evolved from past courses and present experiences in the classroom. I experimented frequently. I did not always use an activity presented here and some which I only used once or twice and found them wanting for some reason are not included here. For example, in the early years of the course, I had an activity on differences in birth order within a family, but as newer research grew to counter the significance of these effects, I dropped the topic entirely.

In my past publications for teachers (Cooperman & Rhoades, 1982, Rhoades & Bradeen-Knox, 1992), I used a traditional lesson-plan format, with activities by title, a rationale, objectives, instructional steps, and comments. If my use of such manuals is typical, I scan the contents and go to the activities that I can easily incorporate into my existing courses. The writing style I adopted for this publication, as you may have identified by now, has a more conversational tone. This publication is more than a how-to teach manual about relationships. It is also a story of the experiences of students who took this course. I chose this in keeping with the spirit of a relationship, a communication from me the writer, to you, the reader. To keep this conversation from being one-sided, feel free to email me with your thoughts, reactions, questions, ideas, or critiques at chuckrhoades@comcast.net.

Chapter 1

Starting Out

Building a Relationship with Youth Participants

Working with a group of adolescents involves developing a relational experience together. The initial sessions begin to build relationships between the students and the instructor, among the students themselves, and among the group as a whole. The creation of these relationships starts when the first student walks in the door. Greet them with a smile, a hello, and a fist-bump or handshake. Ask their name and what they prefer to be called and repeat it back to them, telling them you're glad they are in the group and that you look forward to working with them.

Invite youth to choose their own seat among the chairs and individual tables that are arranged in a circle. Youth typically sit near a person they know. If they don't, introduce them to each other. Sometimes a student sits outside the circle, at an extra place on the periphery. Invite them to sit inside. If they resist, recognize their choice but insist they move, telling them that the circle is the workspace in the class.

Explain that being in the circle facilitates communication in a course that has lots of discussions. In the circle, everyone can see each other. Communication happens with words and also expressions and gestures. Studying relationships involves studying how people communicate.

Respecting the teens means affirming their initial seating choice. You don't know why they chose to sit outside. It might be shyness. It might be because they don't like another youth sitting in the circle. It might be because a new setting is an unsafe space until proven otherwise. The leader's role is to establish and maintain a safe structure in the classroom environment.

While it is important to share some decision-making and power with youth, there is a power differential that will always exist. Teachers assign students' grades. Youth workers in group homes may assign or withhold privileges. The

instructor has the primary responsibility to establish and maintain an environment conducive to the learning process and goals of the course.

Attention to adolescent development involves setting expectations and
boundaries that youth can operate by and rely on. The boundaries give them
something to push against to test their autonomy and also provide safety for
those whose histories of being disrespected or abused require the instructor to
consistently uphold and protect the structure of the group experience.

INTRODUCTIONS

The focus of the initial session should not be on enforcing rules, but on initiating a style of interaction that builds trust, constructive risk-taking, and an
openness to each other's experience in this group. Begin by welcoming them
to the course. Use a structured format for introductions and introduce yourself
to model it for them first. Write the directions on a board or project them onto
a screen. For example, *State the name you want others to call you (in schools
also ask them to indicate their name on the official roster), then say the first
word that comes into your mind in response to a word I give you.*

TEXTBOX 1.1. INTRODUCTION WORD BANK

Here is a word list that could be used for this activity:

relationship	valentine	communication	music
breakfast	break-up	character	date
serious	dance	friend	partner
couple	family	love	party
cartoon	hug	jealous	abuse
school	attachment	decision	make out
lovely	problems	book	hook up

Consider carefully whether to ask youth to indicate their preferred pronouns.
This may inadvertently force those who are non-binary or transgender to out
themselves before they may be ready or willing to do so. Encourage students
to call each other by name, offer them the opportunity to state their pronouns
if they wish, or to do so to you privately if they choose to. In schools, only ask
students to state their last name as it appears on the roster, in case their first

name on the roster was a "dead name," that no longer corresponded with their gender identity (Rachel Rhoades, personal communication, June 17, 2022).

If you choose to ask for their pronouns, tread carefully. Some teens may be surprised or confused about being asked this. You might ask the group why they think you asked for their preferred pronouns. You might hear, "What's a pronoun?" Refer to the pronouns you use for yourself. Some youth know that it has to do with gender or gender identity. Affirm their knowledge. Tell them that asking the name they prefer to be called and the pronouns they want to be used are both signs of respect toward them as individuals. Asking the class to hear what they prefer encourages that respect from everybody in the room.

You might write some examples of pronouns on the board or newsprint or project on a screen: she, her, hers, herself; he, him, his, himself; they, their, theirs, themself; and, as an example of gender neutral pronouns, zie, zir, zirs, zirself. Also state that some people prefer not to use pronouns.

EARLY ICEBREAKERS

Continue the introduction phase of group building with a variety of icebreaker activities. Start by having them disclose some low threat information about themselves. Select activities that get some movement going to build energy and release some stress. For example, you ask them to stand up in response to the following statements:

Stand up if . . .
> *You've ever bossed someone*
> *You've never had a class with anyone in this room*
> *You have lived outside the USA*
> *You've ever met someone famous*
> *If you believe the teacher is always right (okay, this is for laughs)*
> *If you play a musical instrument*
> *If you've ever been in a romantic relationship*
> *If you are in a relationship now*

Their responses to these statements can be helpful to know. If they've never had a class with anyone else in the room, you may give special attention to linking that youth with others. If they've lived outside the United States, they may be able to offer special cultural insights at some points in the course. If they've been in a romantic relationship, or are currently in one, you can surmise that they will be using these filters at some point in the course.

There will probably be youth who enter into and or leave relationships during the program. It may occur among students within the course itself, although that is surprisingly rare. Try to deflect youth from using a class-mate's relationship experience or history as content for the course. Do not put students on the spot to disclose their experiences.

Reassure those currently in relationships that you will not call on them to disclose. Caution them to consider the ramifications of bringing personal information into group discussions. This includes bringing up emotional content that they or others in the class may not really want to deal with in this setting. Clarify that the course is for learning about relationships and that examining one's own experiences in depth are better situated in a counseling format.

Make a statement about boundaries such as this example.

It is important to know what is your business that should be kept private and what you and your partner think is okay to talk about in class. Respect that. The course is not about YOUR relationships, it's an academic study of relationships, but in discussions sometimes students bring up own experiences. Be careful. Think about what you want to say and what you don't want to say.

Offer to meet with any students who wish to talk about issues or concerns that affected or disturbed them in the class. If you are not a trained counselor, keep those one-on-one meetings brief and limited. If you are not a therapist, do not assume the responsibilities of one. Refer students to therapists or counselors. In your brief one-to-one private sessions, just hear them out, use reflective listening, affirm their feelings, and suggest talking to others, including a parent, or recommend readings or journaling.

While icebreakers may seem trivial and little more than playing games, they serve to gradually provide youth with shared experiences vital to building companionship, mutual respect, and trust. These are vital underpinnings for the more sensitive topics coming later in the program.

Ask the students to think of examples of relationships from a movie, book, TV show, or real life couple (not anyone from the school). They could be romantic, parent-child duos, friendships, or other pairings. Give a marker to a teen and have them write a pair on the board, then ask them to pass the marker on to another youth to write another couple, and then they pass it on. Have a few markers in circulation at once. Youth typically listed a variety of couples, from Bert and Ernie to Beyoncé and Jay-Z to the president and first lady (or first gentleman someday).

After generating a dozen or so pairs, facilitate a discussion by asking:

What do these couples have in common?
Which would you consider healthy relationships?
What is it that makes them healthy?

After soliciting ideas about healthy relationships, point out that one of the program goals is to define and determine what makes up a healthy relationship. The list of qualities they offer is a step in that effort.

GROUP AGREEMENTS

Talk about how you want to interact as a group. Some group leaders use terms like *ground rules* or *participation guidelines*. Others prefer *Group Agreements* to connote a jointly derived list of principles that you are all agreeing to and will be responsible for. *Group Principles* would work too!

Taking the time to develop and discuss this list is a crucial part of the initial sessions. It establishes a code of conduct and the expectations that you have for each other. It is a safety net. Giving students a voice in creating the agreements demonstrates that the power and the responsibility of maintaining consistency and fidelity is a shared responsibility among all. The agreements provide a touchstone, a reference point for your interactions, a guide for how you treat each other.

Begin by asking the youth to offer suggestions for the group agreements based on what they see is needed for everyone to participate freely in the course. Do not offer "comfortable" as a guideline for the list, since sometimes the learning experience calls for people to go outside of their comfort zones. The question is really how to make it safe for people to do so.

Your role in the discussion is to encourage student recommendations, to explore in depth what each suggestion means to everyone so that you have a common understanding before you seek consensus or agreement. Contribute your own suggestions based on your experience of working with youth.

Here is a sample list developed in a youth group home:

Anything said in the classroom will be held in confidence, except for issues related to mandatory reporting

We will respect and celebrate our differences and similarities

We will actively and positively participate in our class sessions and leave room for the participation of all

We will respect each person's right to privacy; the right to pass exists if we feel uncomfortable responding to questions

We will avoid using names when relating stories or examples

We will listen to each other; we won't interrupt, distract, or be inattentive

We will be honest with each other

We may add or modify these principles as needed.

Creating the list should take a substantial amount of time. When the group completes the list, ask them to individually indicate that they agree with it by raising their hands. State that it is okay not to agree and that you can continue to discuss the list until you reach consensus. Emphasize that you can revise the list as needed. Assure them that you will check how you are doing in regard to these principles throughout the program.

In subsequent sessions, greet the youth with smiles and their preferred names as they enter the room. Briefly recap the previous session and display the group agreements. Your check-in on the agreements can include questions such as

Are we still okay with these? Do you want clarification on any? Any suggested changes?

CONTINUE GROUP BUILDING

To continue your group building and to get some energy churning in the room, use an adapted version of the classic *Are You Someone Who . . . ?* icebreaker (Simon et al., 1972). Introduce it by modeling the process for the students. Take the signature sheet (Textbox 1.2) and walk up to a student and ask a question from the list.

Are you someone who has read a book about relationships?

If they say no, choose another item until you find one they can say yes for. Ask for their autograph on the signature sheet (you can tell them it will be even more valuable one day after they become famous). Then invite them to ask you a question from the sheet. Distribute the sheets to the other students and instruct them to try to get as many signatures as possible. They can't sign their own sheet and a classmate can only sign once on theirs.

This exercise generates energy as the students move around the room. Everyone gets involved. More extraverted students approach the shyer ones, relieving some pressure to initiate. Encourage them to talk about the items as they mingle. After they collect the signatures invite them to return to their seats. Talk about what was easiest to sign for, what was most difficult and why. Ask how many learned something new about a classmate. They will all raise their hands. Learning something about a person is a step in building a relationship.

Respecting Emotions

Students need guidance to expand their understanding of their own and others' emotional experiences. A relationships course can provide many opportunities for students to learn from their own emotional reactions to activities,

TEXTBOX 1.2. ARE YOU SOMEONE WIIO . . .

Ask questions until the person can sign for something. A person can only sign your sheet once.

1. Has read a book about relationships _____
2. Has seen a movie about a relationship _____
3. Bought a date a meal _____
4. Was treated to a movie on a date _____
5. Has ever been in love _____
6. Broke up in a kind and respectful way _____
7. Wrote someone a love letter _____
8. Texted someone to indicate attraction _____
9. Posted relationship status on social media _____
10. Has babysat for an infant _____
11. Cooked someone a romantic dinner _____
12. Made up after a conflict with a partner _____
13. Supported a friend whose partner was unfaithful _____
14. Initiated a break-up _____
15. Is likely to marry someday _____
16. Knows how birth control pills work _____
17. Had a friend tell someone you were interested _____
18. Likes their parent(s) or guardian(s) _____
19. Started a relationship at a party _____
20. Is a thoughtful partner _____
21. Would rather give a gift than receive one _____
22. Has written a poem about a relationship _____
23. Learned from a past relationship _____
24. Told a secret of yours to a partner _____

discussions, films, and ideas. They can develop an understanding about how feelings happen and that some are enjoyable and comfortable to have and some might be disturbing or uncomfortable.

Youth can learn to identify their feelings and regard them as learning opportunities. You can encourage them to be aware of their emotional experiences during the course and consider not only what the emotion is, but what caused it to occur, and what message it tells about what they are experiencing in that moment. Thinking about what's going on with others emotionally fosters understanding and can help build a relationship.

A tool to use to help identify emotions and emotional intensity is the Feeling Thermometer. Many counselors use such a tool in their therapy sessions and many teachers post it in their classrooms. There are many versions available on-line. You can explain it and ask a youth in the group volunteer to create one for the class.

Introduce the Feeling Thermometer by posting a large model on the wall and distribute a smaller copy to each person. Explain that it shows a range

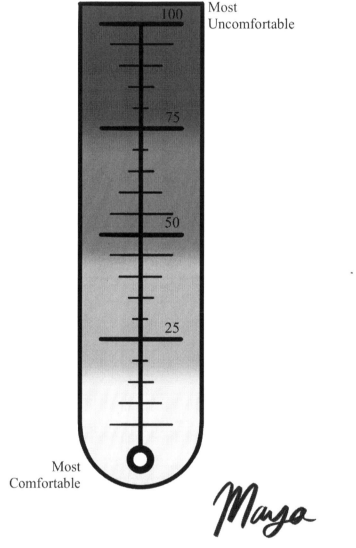

Figure 1.1.   The Feeling Thermometer.

from zero to a hundred, with 100 representing the most discomfort a person is experiencing: extreme anger, anxiety, excitement, nervousness, or other upset. The lower numbers, down to zero, stand for degree of calmness, relaxation, being at peace.

Teach them how to use it with an example. Suppose a person is walking down the street and a large Doberman jumps out unexpectedly from behind a bush, barking angrily.

What might that person's feeling thermometer be showing?

Suppose a person is lying on a quiet beach on a warm day. What might that reading be?

Ask them where they would place the thermometer reading for other examples such as going to a party where you don't know many of the people, being dared to use a substance you're not sure about, being made fun of for something you said in a class, getting an A you didn't expect, failing your driver's test.

How might high and low Feeling Thermometer readings affect people's abilities to deal with these situations?

After they seem to be familiar with the tool, do the first feeling thermometer reading as a group. Ask each youth to give a number for their emotional state at that moment. Relating this activity to the group agreements shows how these tools go together to help individuals adjust to being in the class.

How are our group agreements working?

Do we need to make any revisions based on our experience with the Feeling Thermometer?

ESTABLISHING A NORM OF INCLUSION

The meaningful inclusion of all members is implicit in any well-functioning group. This is especially crucial in adolescent groups, where acceptance by peers is so pertinent developmentally. The group agreements make the principle of inclusion explicit, but to make inclusion a reality, it must be worked on. Doing so at the start of the group experience can set a tone that carries forward to future sessions.

An adaptation of Kathy Obear's *Let Me In*! (1981) activity focuses on inclusion. Developed for a college-level workshop challenging homophobic attitudes and behaviors, the activity uses physical movement to illustrate exclusion and inclusion. Ask for three volunteers (four if there are more than 20 in the class) who start outside a circle formed by the remaining students. Volunteers are usually students with a higher degree of self-confidence, though if there is some hesitancy, ask students who exhibit this trait from the earlier activities (those who initiated contacts for the "Are You Someone Who" activity, for example).

Instruct the other students to form a circle facing inwards. Their task is to keep the outside students from breaking into their circle. Establish ground rules.

No hitting, biting, or kicking—try not to hurt anyone. But keep them out.

Tell the outside volunteers to try to break in. Signal them to try, one at a time, for a minute, and then time it so that they would be joined by another volunteer, then after a minute, by the third.

Choose the smallest volunteer to go first. They will struggle and usually are unable to break into the circle on their own. Sometimes they will scout out the weakest link in the circle or somebody might let them in. More often, the students in the circle tighten and resist with a growing determination.

After a minute, cue the second volunteer to join. Again, the duo will usually be rebuffed by the group. Sometimes the pair succeeds. Sometimes the students on the outside confer before attempting, plotting a strategy.

After another minute, cue the third student. Usually, the trio will find a way to break through the circle. Students go under, through, and even over the top to achieve entry. Carefully monitor the action to prevent injuries.

Process the activity by asking:

What was it like to be an outsider?
Where did your feeling thermometer register during the activity?
What was it like to be an insider?
Where did your feeling thermometer register during the activity?
Were their changes in the feeling thermometer as the activity progressed?
(To insiders) *What did you do to keep them out?*
How did it feel when they did get in?
(To outsiders) *What were your strategies for getting in?*
How did it feel when you got inside?
Take the discussion to another level, by generalizing the exercise to real life.
When are students insiders at this school?
When are students here outsiders?
Are there cliques?
How do you think it feels being an insider at this school? An outsider?
What are the advantages and disadvantages of being an insider? An outsider?

Social psychologists frame inclusion and exclusion using the concept of ingroup-outgroup bias (Sumner, 1906). Being an insider can build self-esteem, but does so at the expense of those who are excluded, the others. There is motivation to maintain this difference because it is linked to individual self-esteem and self-worth. The feeling of superiority enhances the ingroup's solidarity. Efforts to maintain ingroup power ramp up whenever there is a perceived threat, such as occurs when they come into contact and conflict with outsiders. Maintaining superiority often involves vilifying the outsiders. This contributes to stereotyping and discrimination, behaviors that keep the outsiders out and ingroup strong.

Continue deeper into these issues.

A measure of the learning in this class will be seeing how well we can be inclusive.

What can we do to make this happen?

How do we maintain a class environment where everyone here is inside the group?

Which of the agreements we made do you think is especially important for helping us be inclusive of all?

As the adult facilitator in the room, it is your job to pay attention to group process and to the experience each youth is having in the group. The feeling thermometer check-in helps structure an element of inclusion into each session, since every participant speaks. Designing and choosing activities and discussion questions should incorporate awareness to include all. Speaking in language that includes all perspectives in the room, whether by gender, race, ethnicity, or other identity is required of the leader and models the behavior for the students. Inviting students by name to respond to questions can be effective, providing it is done respectfully and gently.

LEARNING NAMES

Youth enter an empty classroom and fill it with their presence, their energy, and whatever back story they bring with them that day. The experience in these sessions provides them with an island of safety and a sense of common purpose during their time together. Think of this and it is easy to smile at them as they enter in anticipation of your work together.

Remember to start off each session with a feeling temperature reading. Ask them to simply state a number on the Feeling Thermometer that corresponds to their current state. Refrain from commenting. Your unspoken message is that feelings are what they are. Just let them be.

Sometimes youth need help learning each other's names. Calling each other by name is a necessary component of group building. Use an activity that accomplishes this and also functions as an energizer. Ask them to stand in a circle. Hold a Nerf ball in your hands and explain that you will throw it to someone in the circle, say their name, and make a wish for them, like *"Jamie, I hope you have a good belly laugh today"* or the generic *"Chris, I hope you have a nice day."* That person will then toss the ball to a different student, say that person's name along with a wish for them. That student tosses it to the next and so on. Emphasize that they are to remember who they received the ball from and who they toss it to.

After completing the round, tell them that now you will toss the ball, in the same order, without speaking to see how well you can do this as a group. Complete the second round. For round 3, ask them to pass the ball a little faster, to see if they can step up their energy and focus. When the third student catches the ball, toss in another Nerf ball. Things get interesting as you keep adding Nerf balls (five or six). When the balls get back to you, keep the tossing alive for a bit longer. There will be misses and drops and people get hit (that's why you use soft balls) and laughter.

Do a Feeling Thermometer check-in, again without comment. Tell them that you are not commenting because you want to allow them to freely state whatever they are feeling at the moment without being concerned about the teacher's reaction or expectations. Your message is that wherever they are at the moment they state their "temperature," is valid and worthy of respect. That is the message in your silence.

After the session's icebreaker, review the group agreements and ask if there is a need for clarification or revision.

INTRODUCE MEDITATION

Select a session early in the program to introduce the practice of meditation. Once started, begin every subsequent session with a brief guided meditation. To set up the first meditation practice, talk about the importance of being aware of the relationship they have with their own selves. To pay attention to your emotional state, as occurs with the Feeling Thermometer readings, is one way to do this. To be in a healthy relationship with others, it is important to have a heathy relationship, and acceptance and appreciation of yourself, your feelings, your abilities, your interests, your hopes and dreams, and to see yourself as worthy of respect.

So, we will start each session from now on by taking time for ourselves individually. We will do this together, so that in our focus on ourselves individually, we are not alone.

We will start each session with a meditation. It is a practice that some cultures have been doing for thousands of years. It is a time for us to take a break from the busyness of daily life and to just be with ourselves.

Ask if any of them have meditated and what they can tell us of that experience. Then proceed step-by-step into the meditation practices. The Power Source program (Casarjian & Casarjian, 2003), originally developed for use with incarcerated youth, begins with simple techniques to build familiarity with the meditative practice.

One such activity is the bell exercise, which involves the use of a bell or chime. You ring a bell and ask the youth to raise their hands when they can no longer hear the sound. Some hands shoot up in a second or two; others join as the sound dissipates. Ring the bell again. The same result will likely occur.

Next ask them to sit comfortably and close their eyes. If they are uneasy having their eyes closed, suggest that they look down and focus on a spot below them. Ring the bell three times. Usually, there is more of a delay before all the hands go up. Talk about the experience.

What was that like for you?
What did you notice?
Were you aware of other sounds?
Were you able to refocus on the bell?
How were you able to do that?
To what extent can you control where your attention goes?
Can you shift your attention?

Ask if they had a different experience with their eyes closed and if so, what they noticed about that. Explain that this first practice in learning meditation is about being able to place their attention where they want it to go. Invite any questions or comments.

In future sessions, begin with the bell to signal the start of the daily meditation. You might let the students take turns ringing it to initiate the experience.

GROUP BUILDING WITH POETRY

Tapping into students' creativity provides another path to building group cohesion. This activity is adapted from one developed by educator Jackie Gerstein (1999). Youth work in groups to create poems about relationships.

Divide the youth into groups of three, situating the trios away from each other for more space and some privacy. Disburse them so that they are in groups different from their chosen seating arrangements. This way, you give them opportunity to make new connections and you can see how they work together with different people. Give each group a packet of 2"x3" slips of paper, on which you wrote short, random words or phrases ("The janitor said," "Gazed out the window," "feeling sleepy," "music blaring,") and others. Have about 25 words cards in each pack, with about ten blank papers for students to write their own words on. Their task is to use the slips of paper to create a poem about relationships. It could be about anything they consider to reflect a theme on relationships.

Give them about 20–30 minutes to complete the task. They then visit each other's work sites, to read the poetry. Have them record what they thought the message or messages about relationships were being presented in each poem. After they complete the circuit, sit down in the circle and talk about it.

Ask each group to read their poem and then ask other members of the class to tell them what message they got from it. It's not about whether they think it was good or bad, or they like it or not, but a deeper comment on the meaning of the poem. Then have the original group indicate what message they sought to present.

After finishing, ask the entire class if they heard any recurrent themes in the poems. Explain that in the course, you will examine different perspectives on relationships, from scientific studies and theories to the arts. This process gives them different ways to access their thinking about relationships.

Students work well in these groups with relatively unfamiliar classmates. Since the task involves them seeking common ground in creating a group poem, they engage in generating ideas, offering suggestions, and receiving feedback. Mingle actively with the groups, giving positive reactions to their work and explicitly asking how they are working together. You want them to tune into the process as well as the content of the activity.

In past courses, students developed a variety of strategies for this task. One group decided to create individual poems as stanzas for the group poem. In another, they took turns adding a line to their poem. Several spread the slips of paper across several desks, discussed possible themes emerging, phrases they liked, and then got to work creating their verses. One group began with a line that intrigued them, and then added lines as they proceeded, an organic process that led them to an unforeseen destination. Some began with a romantic couple in mind, and then chose their lines to fit this preconception. Some identified a tone they wanted, such as humor, and wrote accordingly.

While the primary objective of the activity is to foster connection and contribute to groupbuilding, the content provokes curiosity and anticipation. You all can enjoy and appreciate their cooperative products.

GROUP BUILDING CHALLENGE

Psychologist Gordon Allport (1954) suggested that an effective approach to reduce prejudice is by having members of disparate groups work together to complete a challenging task. His contact hypothesis can be applied as a group-building strategy as well. This activity is adapted from work by educator Craig Dobkin (1999).

In preparation for this activity, tape colored yarn into a large square on the floor. Move all desks and chairs aside. Tell them that the task is to accomplish a series of challenges that become increasingly difficult as they proceed. Divide the group equally on each of the 4 sides and have them stand with both feet on the yarn.

The first task is to keep both feet on the yarn for a count of six.
Count to six and congratulate them for their accomplishment.
Are you ready for the next challenge?

They will want you to bring it on. Instruct them to move around the room and return to the same spot that they are on now. Any foot on the floor must be touching the yarn or the whole group has to start over. They will do this easily. Praise their effort.

Are you ready for another challenge?

They will confidently and maybe a little scornfully assure you they are ready. Ask each youth to each point to a spot directly across from where they are standing.

Move to that spot without stepping off the yarn.

At first it seems easy but they quickly realize they have to help each other in order to follow the rules of having both feet on the yarn when their feet are on the ground. Some groups experience their first "do-over" at this task. But they all get it done.

Are you ready for the next challenge?

At this point, their growing confidence is accompanied with a sense that this could get more difficult, as you predicted at the start. Assign each side of the square a number (1, 2, 3, 4) sequentially in clockwise order. Challenge Sides 1 and 2 to switch places with each other so that each person is in the same place on that side that they were on their original spot. Again, any foot on the floor has to be touching the yarn or the whole group has to start over.

Then have Sides 3 and 4 switch. This gets more complicated as they have to step over and around each other. There are often "do-overs" at this stage. After they succeed, I commend them and ask, *Are you ready for the next challenge?*

They will probably respond affirmatively but warily. In the next challenge, have Sides 1 and 3 and 2 and 4 switch. This is actually really simple, since all they have to do is walk around the square. Some groups get this quickly; others struggle. They invariably laugh when they discover the solution.

Nicely done. Are you ready for the next challenge?

The camaraderie becomes apparent as they affirm their readiness. Distribute bandanas or actual blindfolds (from a party store) to every other student and task them to move around the square and return to the starting position. Holding hands tends to be the strategy of choice. Almost every group has to start over during this phase as one or more blindfolded student steps off the yarn. The group discovers that they have to talk more or even assist each other by guiding a blind classmate's step by touch. They usually can do it, though.

Way to go! Are you ready for the next challenge?

They give a determined but very wary *"Yes."* *Every* student gets a blindfold. Tell them to move around the square and return to their starting point. This gets very interesting and most, but not all groups, figure out how to succeed. There are many do-overs. Some strategies youth adopted involved taking off the shoes so that could better feel the yarn, squatting around the square and using their hands to feel the yarn, and posting the last in the line to stand by the corner so that the next line knows where to turn. Some cheat by peeking.

Since you need time to discuss the activity, limit the number of attempts by number or by time. If they succeed, praise them. If they don't, praise them. Their effort was what counted. Discuss the process.

> *What do you think was the purpose of the activity?* (They get this—to work together, to learn how to work together, to build cohesion, togetherness.)
> *What did you notice about how the group worked?* (They typically judge themselves on their successes and note the importance of helping each other.)
> *How did individuals help the group function?* (They identify roles that individuals assumed, noting that some emerged as leaders; others as caretakers.)
> *How did individuals make it more difficult for the group to do its tasks?*

If conflicts or disagreements occurred, talk about it. Ask them to discuss how the conflicts were resolved and how the entire group behaved during the conflict. You might discuss different ways to deal with conflict and issues like exerting power over another, forming opposing groups, or working toward compromise or consensus. Encourage them to view conflicts and disagreements as learning opportunities to be done with caring and respect for each other. Let them know that you will be addressing conflict in more detail later in the course.

Do you feel any differently about being in the group (class) after the activity? (Most reported this as a positive experience and sensed a closeness building with their classmates.)

SHARING SELF-DISCOVERY

Psychologist Erik Erikson (1963; 1968) developed a theory that our lives are lived in eight distinct stages and that at each stage we experience a psychological conflict that we have to resolve. In infancy, the conflict is trust versus mistrust. An infant learns the fundamentals of trust when their caregiver holds them when they cry, feeds them when they're hungry, and changes their diaper when they're wet. When these actions do not regularly occur, the child has more difficulty learning to trust that their needs will be met.

In adolescence, Erickson said that the task was identity versus role confusion. He explained that up to this stage development mostly depends upon what people do for us or to us. Beginning in adolescence, development depends primarily upon what we do. People's lives become more complex in the attempt to establish one's own identity, struggle with social interactions, and reflect on moral issues.

The adolescent task is to discover the individual self that is separate from family (or families) of origin and as members of a wider society. The central question is *Who are we and what is our place in the world?* Being unsuccessful in navigating this stage results in confusion and dismay.

Facilitate self-exploration by asking them to write down ten answers to the question, "Who am I?" Ask them to read all items to the class and again whip around the room with the readings.

What did you notice about how people identified themselves?

Typically some categories emerge, with students identifying themselves by roles they assume (athlete, band member), their relationships (brother, sister, friend), traits (happy, careful), or skills (a good listener, smart).

What are some things you've heard others say about you? Are any of these on your list?

What are some roles that you act out in your life?

You may need to help them by stating that we may act differently in different situations, circumstances, or with different people.

How do you think acting in these roles affects our identity?

This sometimes came off as a "which is first, the chicken or the egg?" discussion.

Does being a musician define oneself or is one's musical interest and aptitude cause us to become musicians? Does it matter? Getting to recognize that how we act may shape our self-perceptions is the point here. Because we find ourselves in different situations with different people and then act differently than in other situations, the question for you is

Do we have a core self that we maintain throughout all our various experiences?

To summarize, the opening sessions serve to inform the youth about what the course entails, establish agreements for how you will function as a group, and lay the groundwork for future sessions by building trust and mutual respect among group members.

Chapter 2

Fostering Growth and Safety through Structure and Routine

As you move forward in the group-building stage, students will continue to gain familiarity with each other and the group process you are establishing. They tend to take the same seats, even if you do not assign seating. This shows their need for consistency, structure, continuity, and comfort.

Maintaining structure throughout the sessions provides continuity and regularity that the students can depend on. This is especially important for students with trauma histories, whose healing processes can be supported with such clarity and predictability. It aids other students as well in that the structure provides parameters for the process. When you start each session with a meditation, for example, students will quiet down and focus on the experience. This practice smoothly helps them segue immediately into the next learning activity. Over time you will find that if you forget or deliberately omit the meditation, students will call you out for what they see as an infraction. Yield to their wisdom.

USING THE GROUP AGREEMENTS

Checking in on the group agreements regularly becomes an important way to bring the teens' attention to your group process. Refer to the list by showing on the screen or post it on newsprint and ask if the agreements are working and if any additions or changes are needed. Remind them of the importance of the group agreements, perhaps mentioning the *Let me In* activity that had introduced it. Their attention to the agreements holds themselves, their classmates, and you, their instructor, to the same standards of conduct that you all determined to be the best way you wanted to interact with each other. This attention to group agreements helps prevent many problems and when issues do arise, it gives everyone a common reference for working things through.

19

Call attention to the group agreements whenever something happens in class when you sense it is appropriate and helpful. If a student discloses something that you perceive exposes vulnerability, thank the student for their statement and interject a reminder about the group agreement on confidentiality. If a student uses another student's name that was not present in the class, remind them of the "no names" guideline.

Sometimes you might wonder whether they are seeing a group agreements issue that you notice, so ask, *"Does anyone see whether we need to apply the group agreements to what just happened/what was just said?"*

If you sense that attention to group agreements would enhance or be important to keep in mind for an upcoming activity, simply note that you'll be working to apply the agreements during this next activity and give a reason for that instruction.

> *Folks can have different opinions about what we're going to be talking and about and sometimes strong emotions get stirred up, so let's be sure to listen well, listen to understand, and respect each other as we do this.*

The regular check-ins to evaluate your adherence to the agreements involve asking:

> *Which of the agreements are we doing really well with?*
> *Which agreements do you think we need to pay more attention to?*

Another regular practice is to commend them for their efforts in adhering to the agreements.

While providing a dependable, reliable, clear structure for our class interactions, the group agreements also function as a way to build trust and validate students' experiences within the group. This is especially important for students who have been marginalized in the school or community, or even within their own homes. The structure provides an element of predictability and safety for students surviving traumatic experiences. You are providing a safety net or safe space for students.

Mindfulness

To lead adolescents in meditation and other mindfulness activities, it is important that you, the instructor become familiar by engaging in such practices on your own. While there are personal preferences on how to do this, it is important to do so regularly, daily if possible. Taking a class or training can get you started. There are many on-line resources, apps, and organizations that offer instruction and guided meditations. There are opportunities for meditating in a group in many communities. You will benefit personally by meditating and also be better accomplished at leading mindfulness practices with youth.

With meditation there is a sustained concentration that grows with practice, a calmness that derives from attention to one's inner experience of the present, on one's breath or movement or attention to a guided visualization. You can develop a fuller understanding of mindfulness based on the writings of Thich Naht Hanh (1976) who defines it as being wholly in the present moment. Jon Kabat-Zinn (1999; 2012) has written and recorded helpful works on how to meditate. Psychologist Sam Himelstein (2013) provides insights on how to lead meditations with youth experiencing trauma.

There can be a range of experience with mindfulness practices in any given class. Starting together with introductory exercises helps you go forward as a group. Some students take to meditation quickly, especially those with prior experience. Assure those that are hesitant or reluctant that it is okay to have those reactions, but ask them to give it a try. It is fine to sit and have a quiet time if they choose not to participate in the formal meditation. Sitting and being quiet is itself consistent with the meditation time.

Giving options to participate or just sit quietly is especially important for youth who have experienced trauma. It gives them a sense of control that the trauma took away. Some may choose to meditate with the group once the option to abstain has been offered. Others do what they think is best for them. Check in with them individually to see how they're doing with the meditation time.

Research on Meditation

In classes where there is initial resistance or hesitancy about meditating, it can help to provide information on its effects from research findings. A convincing argument comes from a meta-analysis of 47 studies on meditation reported by researchers at Johns Hopkins University which found that meditation improved outcomes for depression, anxiety, pain management, stress, and mental health-related quality of life (Goyal et al., 2014). A mental health curriculum developed for New Beginnings, an agency serving homeless youth in Maine that included meditation in every session found improvements in participants' emotional intelligence, particularly in self-awareness and stress management (Rhoades, Pierce-Glover, & Ruchinskas, 2017). Do a review of articles in psychological journals using the PsycNet database from the American Psychological Association for current studies.

Meditation Practices

Introduce the use of meditation as a daily practice. Start slowly, with simple examples and step-by-step guidance, incorporating meditation as the first activity of each session. When the meditation chime, bell, or listening bowl sounds, it signals the youth to begin to sit comfortably, close their eyes (or look down), and take a deep cleansing breath. Guide them through these steps, with a similar repetition each time. After time, you may find it interesting that if you deviate from this, even in a very minor way, eyes will open and a student will call you out on your error. It is like you are conducting an orchestra of breathers who knew the score as well as you.

Invite them to sit comfortably, close their eyes or look down, and bring their attention to their breathing. Use a gentle, calm voice throughout the meditation practices. Ask them to take a *cleansing breath*.

> *Inhale and fill your lungs so that your stomach puffs out a little. Hold the air in briefly, then completely empty your lungs. Blow out so that your stomach is flat. Let's do it again.*

Tell them to bring their attention to the air coming in and going out.

> *If you are distracted by a sound, a noise, an itch, or a thought, that is normal. It's okay. Just notice it, then in your mind tell it goodbye, and return your attention to your breathing.*

Continue to direct their attention to their breathing.

> *Watch the air come into your body. Are you breathing through your nose or mouth or both? You don't have to control anything; your body knows how to breathe. Feel your diaphragm as it fills with air and bumps your belly out a little. Notice how the air is cool when it enters and warmer when you exhale. Just pay attention to your breathing. If you're distracted by a sound, a noise, a body sensation like an itch, or a thought that comes into your mind, it's okay. That's normal. Just notice it, then mentally say goodbye to it and return your attention to your breathing.*

After a minute or two, you can ascertain that they have entered a calm state and you can begin a guided meditation that lasts for 5–10 minutes, sometimes longer.

Talk about how the meditation is going, especially in the early weeks. Validate student experiences of being distracted during meditation by stating that this happens to everyone and that you experience it when you meditate. Assess their willingness to try something that can help and that they can do by and for themselves. Encourage them to meditate outside of the group and maintain a record of their experiences (Casarjian & Casarjian, 2013).

Some students have difficulty beginning meditation because they view it as another academic task, which brings with it a self-imposed pressure to perform and perform well. Try to ease this stress by telling them that the spirit of meditation is about *being* more so than *doing*.

Our meditations are times when you can take a break from the daily grind, the work, the demands you face. This is your time, when you can just be with yourself. You don't have to be anywhere or do anything except breathe and pay attention to your present experience.

Meditation Tools

A chime, bell, or singing bowl serves well to signal the start and end of a meditation practice. Besides this function, it is a physical manifestation of the structure and routine you are establishing in the group.

While they are often inaccurate at their designed purpose of measuring stress levels, Biodots can be useful to aid in early meditation practices (Lowenstein, 2015). The 1/4-inch circles are placed in the webbing of the hand between the thumb and index finger. An instructional card accompanies the dot to help students identify their stress levels by color, which ranges from violet for relaxed to black for stressed, with the midpoints being green for tense and turquoise for alert.

Ask the students to think of something irritating to attempt a stress rating to demonstrate how to read the Biodots. Some will see this happen; others might not notice any changes. Then test whether meditating affects the color of the dot. After leading them through a practice, check the Biodots again and see if there is a change. Typically half will see movement toward the relaxation mark. Some might report that they felt more relaxed after the meditation but their Biodot didn't reflect that. The usefulness of the Biodots does not lie in their measurement capacity so much as in bringing students' attention to how meditation might reduce stress levels and engender relaxation.

A more accurate, though more expensive, device is the Muse headband (InteraXon, 2021). The EEG instrument measures brain waves and can provide accurate feedback on brain activity during meditation. The Muse program (InteraXon, 2021) guides the wearer in deepening their meditation practice. If you obtain one or two, you can have the youth take turns over the sessions.

Other useful devices for measuring physiological changes are over-the-counter blood pressure cuffs and pulse oximeters, which are available at most pharmacies. A simple timer on a cell phone or watch can help measure pulse rates. The following directions can guide the youth to measure the effect of meditation on their pulse rates.

Some youth enjoy listening to soft music as they meditate. There are many instrumental recordings specifically produced for this purpose and many others work as well (Kvarnstrom & Schramm, 1989; Oliver, 1992; Winter, 1997).

> *We're going to bring our hearts to this meditation practice today. Literally bring our hearts. The heart is more than just a pump; it communicates all kinds of information to our brains. It feeds blood to our brains.*
>
> *First, find your pulse, where an artery passes close to the surface of the skin, like at your wrist or our neck. Let's try the wrist. Hold one of your hands out with the palm facing up. Place two fingers, your index (pointer) and middle finger on the inside of your wrist below the base of your thumb. Touch your wrist lightly with the two fingertips. Can you feel your pulse? If you can't, touch with a little more pressure or move your fingers around a little.*
>
> *If you can't find it on your wrist, try your neck. Press the same two fingers on the side of your neck beside your Adam's apple in the hollow area, like this* (demonstrate). *That's your carotid artery.*
>
> *Count how many beats there are over a 20-second period. I'll time you. Ready, count.* (Pause for 20 seconds.) *Okay, stop. Now multiply what you counted by 3. That gives you your heart rate per minute.*

Sample Meditation Scripts

Start each meditation with the same basic instruction by asking them to sit comfortably, close their eyes or look down, and take a deep cleansing breath. If they seem restless, have them take another cleansing breath. Have them direct their attention to their breathing, observing how the air moves into and out of their nose or mouth and how their lungs fill and empty.

Pause for a minute or two to allow the youth to establish a rhythm to their breathing and to enter a meditative state. Then use a guided meditation for their daily practice. There are many guided meditation scripts on-line and in publications, in print and recorded (Boyle, 1993; Brotman et al., 2005; Casajarian, 2016; Casajarian & Casajarian, 2003; Chudnofsky, et al., 2014; Heller, 2015; Lusk, 1992, 1993; Schwartz, 1995). Read and practice speaking a script before bringing it to your group.

Here is a favorite of many students who enjoyed the calm feelings it engendered, especially when they are experiencing hectic times in their daily lives. It comes from the Zen Buddhist tradition and is thought to be centuries old (Bob Karnan, personal communication, April 12, 1987). Proceed with a slow cadence, pausing after each punctuation mark to allow the students to create the images that you describe.

Imagine a forest. Dense woods. It is Spring and the leaves are beginning to appear. A stream winds through the forest. The water is high, fed by the Spring rains and the melting of the Winter snows.

The current moves swiftly, powerfully through the woods. A dry leaf, hanging on a branch for months, detaches, and slowly floats down, down to the surface of the water. It is quickly carried out of sight by the strong rush of the stream.

A twig falls down into the stream and it too disappears with the flow.

A pebble drops and breaks through the surface of the water. It descends down, down, down to the bottom. It lodges in the stream bed. Stable and secure. The powerful current washes over it, along both sides, but the pebble doesn't move. It lies still amid the surge.

Focus your attention on the pebble. Feel its strength. Feel its stability. No matter how hard the water moves around and over it, the pebble doesn't move.

In times of stress in your life, when you feel life's currents move fast and powerfully against you, remember the strength and stability of the pebble and how you are connecting to that image right now. Bring this memory to that day and be like the pebble, calm, strong, and secure.

Pause for 1–2 minutes.

When you are ready, bring your attention back to your breathing, then back to this room. Open your eyes or look up and be here now.

You might save this meditation until the students have had at least two weeks' experience with the group meditation. It can be repeated upon request or if there are events happening in the community or the world that create strong currents of unrest, such as reports of a school shooting.

If so inclined, you may write your own script as a special gift to your group. This was written for students in a relationships course at Portsmouth High School during a particularly harsh winter. On February 2 every year, thousands of people, attired in gowns and black tie outfits, gather at sunrise in Punxsutawney, Pennsylvania. They observe whether Punxsutawney Phil, a groundhog, will see his shadow. If he does, it means Phil will retreat to his den to shelter from six more weeks of winter. If he doesn't, Spring will arrive early. That year, there was hope for a cloudy morning.

Lay or sit comfortably. Close your eyes. Breathe deeply.

What would it be like to BE Punxsutawney Phil?

You've been hibernating since October in your cozy burrow in the hills of Indiana County, Pennsylvania, near the small town of Punxsutawney.

Your breathing rate has dropped to 16 beats a minute, way down from the 80 beats per minute when you are awake and active. As you lay asleep, down beneath the earth, you dream groundhog dreams.

You remember your last meal before descending into your warm burrow. Apple peels, yum, beans and peas, clover, dandelions, flowers, the bark of the maple tree (sweet) and a few crunchy insects.

There was that last playing around with Cousin Frieda and Nephew Paulie. Rolling around in the leaves in our furry brown roundness playing groundhog tag and hide and seek. You won the swimming race in the creek.

Then it was time to go and you remember climbing into your own lovely burrow, squeezing through the opening, making your way down using your curved claws to pull forward and short but strong legs to push downward.

A quick pit stop in the bathroom chamber to relieve yourself, then down again to the soft and warm mud bed way below the earth.

Sleeping through October. Sleeping through November. Sleeping through December, January. 16 beats per minute.

February. What's this? Sensing a distant rumbling, you stir. You open your small round eyes and realize you're still in your cozy burrow but something's changed. The ground is shaking ever so slightly. It seems to be increasing. There are other noises too. Unclear sounds. You look up and see a dim light at the top of the burrow.

You climb slowly up to see what's going on. Is it Spring already?

Slowly up up up claws pulling upward, stubby legs pushing upward. Nearing the opening, noisier, brighter. What's going on?

Poke your head out of the burrow and there are thousands of humans! They're all around! Look to the left, people. To the right, people. Behind you see your shadow and the people erupt in cheers and applause and it's for me. Phil Phil Phil.

All right.

Almost worth waking up for. But I'm going back to bed.

As you might surmise, meditating does not preclude giggling. In another group, the leader overheard youth comparing superhero movies before the session began. He read this script for the next day's meditation.

Picture a superhero. Wonder Woman. Batman. Catwoman. Black Panther. Spiderman. Storm. Wolverine. X-Woman Jean Grey. Thor. Superman. Supergirl. The Flash. Black Widow. Hulk. Iron Man. Captain Marvel. Deadpool. Harley Quinn. Northstar. Captain America. Dreamer. Thunder. Lightning.

Maybe you can think of another superhero or create your own.

Who appeals to you? Who has qualities that YOU have? Who has qualities that you WANT to have?

See yourself as having the powers of a superhero. See yourself applying those powers in your own life.

Let yourself fantasize about this. (Pause 2–3 minutes)

Bring your attention back to your breathing. Back to this room. When I ring the chime, come back to class.

Thoughtfully select each day's meditation. Consider the day of the week as they affect student energy levels. Mondays and Fridays tend to be low energy so you may want to use more active scripts. Other criteria include school, community, and world events, group dynamics, and especially, how the meditation relates to the topic or issues you are addressing in the session.

Active Mindfulness

Mindfulness is an umbrella term for meditation and other present-moment focused activities. It involves bringing one's full awareness to what is happening in the present moment. It involves concentration and attention, so we can also be mindful when we are doing other things.

To illustrate this idea, give each youth a small bag of popcorn and instruct them to take one piece out. Guide their process with slow and deliberate instruction. Some instructors use raisins or a potato chip for this classic introductory activity.

> *Look at the piece of popcorn. Don't eat it yet. Get to really examine it. Turn it around and see the different sides. Note the shape, the regular surface and the irregularities, parts that may be sticking out. Roll it in your fingers. Feel its texture. What does it smell like? Does it make a noise? Stick your tongue out and lick it. Taste it. Put it in your mouth but don't chew yet. Let it sit on your tongue. What is that like? Move it around your mouth slowly. Bite down. Again. Chew it up and watch with your mind as you swallow it.*

Some student will giggle through it. Some roll their eyes. Most just get into it. Ask them what they think is the point of doing this. They get it—Being in the here and now.

Use another example to show how practicing mindfulness, even in a brief instance, can help them manage stress. As they sit in their chairs, ask them to see whether they can lower their shoulders. Most sense this existing, but little noticed tension. Discuss how this awareness demonstrates that people can carry a level of stress with them and not know it.

> *Being able to lower our shoulders tells us two things. One, that we are experiencing some, even small level of stress at that moment. Two, by breathing deeply and relaxing our shoulders, we can mitigate that stress.*

Another follow-up to reinforce teaching the concept of mindfulness with some fun is to solicit three volunteers who are comfortable with being stared at. Ask them to pose in the center of the room while their classmates look them over. Accompany the three outside the room and instruct them to change three things about their appearance. Youth can get very creative with this, making some obvious and some very subtle changes to their hair, shoelaces, shirts, and other clothing and accessories. Returning to the classroom, challenge the class to figure out what changes were made. After they discover the changes, ask them what they had to do to accomplish the activity. Being mindful means concentrating awareness and attention.

The students like blowing bubbles as a mindfulness activity. Give each of them a small container and wand and lead them through very slow, one-at-a-time multi-sensory investigation of a bubble's properties. Encourage them to continue the bubble play while you ask questions.

When you blow a bubble, where does it go?
What does it look like?
What do you notice about the size, shapes, color, and number?
It's okay to be distracted by other people's bubbles. Don't judge yourself for getting distracted; just bring your attention back to your own.

Later in the course, after they accumulate mindfulness experiences, take a walk outside. Challenge them to maintain an awareness of their breathing while noticing the array of stimuli available. This exercise can bring awareness to the many sensory signals accessible in their everyday environment. The colors of the building, cracks in the pavement, grass and weeds, bird calls, cloud formations, changing pressure of the breeze, sounds of footsteps, smells of flowers, litter, sidewalk irregularities, and other observations can be made on these walks. Being mindful gives them an opportunity to be in their world in a different way. Perhaps needless to state, ban cell phones during this walk!

Processing this activity by talking about other places and times when mindful attention to the present might occur. They will quickly conclude it can happen virtually anywhere, anytime. To reinforce this discovery in future sessions, ask them about any mindful experiences they had recently. You will hear evidence that the students are transferring their learning outside this course. Some examples students provided were being mindful of their room, their breathing, and the light when they awoke in the morning, letting their wandering minds during a class of waning interest focus on their physical experience of being in the room, sitting on the bench during a sports event, hearing various instruments individually and in combination during a band performance, and sitting still for a brief time while among friends.

Include an active mindfulness exercise frequently in your sessions as practice in mindfulness and to help energize the group. There are many resources for energizers or ice-breakers that can easily be converted into mindfulness activities (Cavert & Frank, 1999; Frazier & Mehle, 2013).

Songs about Relationships

Music is a distinguishing characteristic of a generation. Adolescence is when people form their musical preferences. Songs from these years become a part of "our era." The recognition of tunes from our teenage years forms a bridge of connection that extends far into our lives. It is no wonder that music from teenage years is used as a way of connecting to patients with Alzheimer's. Music impacts our memories, emotions, and our moods then and now (Levitin, 2006).

Including music as a way of examining relationships became a favorite part of the course. Introduce it about halfway through. Students can choose any song about relationships. They can choose any genre. In student groups every genre except opera was heard. They chose contemporary popular songs, country-and-western, hip-hop, and more frequently than expected, songs from the 1960s and 1970s era. The most common themes selected by students centered on heartbreak, rejection, failed relationships, and unrequited love.

In one class, a student wrote his own song especially for the assignment. After graduation this student, Sam Robbins, became a Nashville recording artist.

Establish a rule that lyrics have to be school-appropriate, with no f-bombs or n-words. This is easier than it sounds as YouTube provides "clean" versions of many songs. Use black marker to blot out the taboo words before distributing the lyrics or better, just project the edited words onto a screen in the room.

Assign the students specific days to present their songs in class. Ask them to provide the lyrics so that everyone can follow along. This helps in deciphering lyrics that are difficult to discern. The presenting student then leads a discussion on what the song means to the listeners. Coach them beforehand on how to write open-ended questions to facilitate discussions. They are to prepare three open-ended questions to ask the class. Give them some examples.

> *What does the song say about how to deal with a partner who's unfaithful?*
> *What is your opinion of this message?*
> *What else could a person do when a partner is unfaithful?*
> *What do you think the lyrics "_____" mean?*

Many will model their questioning techniques on those you employ in the class. You may be surprised and think "That's what I sound like!"

Some students worry and feel stressed about leading the class discussions. Some fear that classmates won't like their song. Emphasize that the focus is on the messages about relationships that the song gives and that the subjective liking or disliking of the song itself doesn't matter. Provide them with tips for facilitating the discussions.

Ask open-ended questions.
Allow time for your classmates to think about a question you asked before moving on to the next one. This allows classmates time to think about what you're asking.
Invite students to respond to each other's statements (What did you think about what ___ said?)
Tell us your thoughts about the song at the end of the discussion.

When you first announce the assignment, address their concerns by asking the class what advice they would give a classmate who felt nervous about presenting. They will likely come through with ideas taken from the group agreements and mindfulness practices. You will likely hear "breathe deeply," and promises to be a supportive audience. Work with some students individually when needed. Rather than having any student present alone, schedule their presentation so that two students lead the group each day you do the activity. Schedule them so that one hesitant student is paired with a confident classmate that can work with them to help ease their discomfort. Examine two songs right after the daily meditation. Applaud for each presenter.

Some students bask in the limelight and are excellent facilitators. Some students zoom through their questions, moving on quickly after getting a single response. Since they are all going to be leaders, you will rarely or never hear a put-down or criticism by a peer.

Having the words to the songs to follow along is essential. You may hear some popular songs for the first time so the activity provides you with a glimpse that you lacked. At some point in one's teaching career or youth work you will lose touch with current music. This activity brings it back to you. You may gain an appreciation of current genres. Some songs may dazzle you. In one group, Beyoncé's *If I Were a Boy* (Jean & Gad, 2008) generated a discussion that lasted almost an entire class period.

Poems about Relationships

Continue the investigation of what The Arts can teach about relationships by following the music activities with a look at poetry. Instead of songs, the youth select poems with relationship themes, or if so inclined, write their own verse. This can be either a mini-unit or implemented like the song assignments, with two students presenting their poems over a period of weeks. You can again have the students lead discussions with this task, or simply provide an oral or written report on their view of the poem's messages about relationships.

To model the activity, read selected poems to the class or ask students to volunteer to read them. Project the words onto a screen or distribute hard copies to accompany the reading. Two poems in the public domain that youth enjoyed were it may not always be so . . . by e. e., cummings (1963) and *Sonnet 43: How do I love thee, let me count the ways* by Elizabeth Barrett Browning (1906). Students also enjoyed Gary Soto's *Time with You* (2009).

Read the poems one time through, then read each again, stopping after each poem to discuss it.

What is the poem saying about love and relationships?
What is the poet hoping for?

An important aspect of poetry is word choice. Point out that poets choose their words carefully to present the precise meaning they want in their work. For example, Soto states that clouds roll at "super speed."

How is that different from simply saying "fast?"
What words did the poet choose that stood out for you? Why?

Give the students about 20–30 minutes to find poems online that speak about love and relationships. They could search for these terms or terms like "Valentine's Day poetry" or they could choose particular themes (first love, jealousy, passion) that they might be interested in reading.

The following link can access several different poets: http://famouspoetsandpoems.com/love_poems.html. Instruct them to select any poem they find meaningful to them to bring to class and read on their assigned day. Also give them the option to write their own poem.

To summarize, establishing a structure that offers predictability while providing for examinations of relevant course themes can help to build group cohesion, trust, and security within the group.

Chapter 3

Family

The course focuses primarily on romantic relationships. Laying the groundwork to get there involves first building relationships as a class, as described in chapter 1, and taking a look at the important relationships people have earlier in life, most of which continue into the present. Family, relatives, and friends, past and present, comprise these contacts.

Address the study of families with caution. The purpose here is to study what individuals learned about relationships from these earliest interactions, and how these experiences might affect their later couple relationships. Seek to maintain an academic approach to avoid therapizing youth histories. It is a delicate matter to tread among these topics with students who have been forced out of their homes because of their gender identity or sexual orientation, a parent's drug abuse, sexual abuse, or family violence. Inform the school's guidance department or youth counselors before you begin this unit so that they are aware and ready should students need to talk.

Make the purpose of the unit clear at the outset, acknowledging that there are a range of experiences among families of origin and family constellations. Reassure the teens that no one would be put on the spot to disclose personal histories and that counselors are available to talk to if needed. Inform the students of each session's content at the end of the prior session. Refer to the group agreements regularly and select calming scripts for the meditations.

The other side of family experiences lies in the joy of connection that builds from birth. These connections take place in a variety of circumstances. Some students reside in two-parent families. Some live with a single parent or grandparents or live in two households, alternating between two parents who live separately, often divorced. Students may live with another relative, like an aunt or uncle. Some reside in group homes. Students are living in unhoused situations as well.

Begin the unit by having the students identify the people close to them in their lives at present and what criteria they have for considering closeness.

You will then look back at Erik Erikson's developmental theory (1963; 1968), which identifies the relationships that are most important at each life stage.

From Erikson, move on to Attachment Theory (Bowlby, 1958), which helps students understand how individuals develop styles or patterns of thinking and behavior that influence their participation in later relationships. Point out that even though these influences may be felt, they do not necessarily control how a person develops and maintains relationships in later life. In other words, present the idea that people are not victims of destiny. A person can emerge from insecurity or disorganized or even abusive upbringings into healthy, mutually supportive, and fulfilling relationships.

CLOSENESS OF CONNECTIONS

Begin the discussion of family by identifying where people in their lives fit according to their own sense of closeness. Distribute a blank paper to each youth and ask them to draw a large circle. Have them write their names in the center. Ask them to write the names or other identifier (uncle, aunt, classmate, etc.) for people they feel connected to, placing the names within the circle to indicate how close they view this person to them. For example, close family members and best friends might be next to their name, cousins or a grandparent a little further away, friends like fellow band member or teammates a little further away, classmates they like a little outside of that, and acquaintances near the outside of the circle.

Ask them to think about the closeness of relationships.

When you say a person is close to you, what does that mean?

When they finish, ask the students to work in pairs to share their circle assignments with another person. Then discuss the activity as a group.

What was similar about how you placed people in your diagrams?
What differences did you see?

Ask where they placed the following people and for their reasons for placing them there.

Family members? Friends? Females your age? Males your age? Younger boys and girls? Adult men? Adult women? This group?

Discuss how the degree of closeness affects what is said or done with people.

Who would you want to have fun with?
Who would you tell a secret to?
Who can you most be yourself with?
Who would put you in their closest circle?
Who would you ask for help with a personal problem?
How would a person in an outer circle get into a closer circle?

Relatives

As a follow-up to the circle activity give students an opportunity to examine their connections with relatives. Ask them to draw four columns on a paper. Mark the four columns, Names, Where they live, How often you see them, and How important is your connection to them. These are jumping off points for a small group discussion. Have students complete their lists, then place them into small groups of no more than 3–4 and ask them to talk about their relatives. Follow that with a large group discussion.

What do you notice about your information?
How would you describe your connections to your relatives?
How do you feel about those connections?

Knowing About Our Close Connections

Another activity involves identifying and sharing information about family members and relatives. Introduce the discussion by noting that getting close to people involves developing a history of shared experiences. Closeness brings a tendency for people to know things about each other in ways that are different and more personal, than with other people.

Ask the youth to think about two family members, relatives, or family friends that they feel closest to. Ask them to write down information about these close connections.

Their favorite movie, TV show, or book
A memorable birthday or holiday with them
Their favorite indoor and outdoor activities
A strong belief they have
A sad event you shared with them
A happy event you shared with them

Randomly assign students to talk in pairs about the information on their close connections, elaborating as they wish, and asking each other questions.

Remind them that they are in control of what information they want to talk about and what they choose not to disclose.

Erikson Stages

Begin this session with a brief synopsis of Erikson's (1963, 1968) theory or show a four-minute YouTube video http://www.youtube.com/watch?v =A0sxaU34MPE as an overview. Divide the students into eight groups, providing a brief description of one of Erikson's stages to each group. See https://www.simplypsychology.org/Erik-Erikson.html.

Assign each group a different stage. Instruct them to review the description and prepare a report to give to the class. Tell them to include the name of the stage, the age range, an explanation of the conflict, major life events at that stage, and the relationships that are most important. Suggest that they draw an image on the board or newsprint that depicts their stage. Discuss the activity.

What is an important idea that you learned while engaging in this activity? Why do you believe that this idea is important?
How might knowing about Erikson's stages apply what you learned from this activity to your own life?

Movie Application: *Breaking Away*

The film, *Breaking Away* (Yates, 1979) can be a vehicle to help students apply their learning about Erikson's stages, particularly the adolescent stage, to a film analysis. Watch the movie (and all films you show) beforehand. Identify the characters and encourage the group to think about Erikson's theory as they watch. In some groups, it might help to give the discussion questions in advance of seeing the movie so that they can take notes for the subsequent discussion.

Describe how Dave is experiencing Erikson's Adolescent Stage.
How do Dave's parents react to his identity conflict? Do you think this is typical of most parents? Explain your answer.
Cyril said, "I was sure I was going to get that scholarship. My dad of course was sure I wasn't. When I didn't, he was real understanding, you know. He loves to do that. He loves to be understanding when I fail." How did his father's attitude toward him affect Cyril in his childhood years, according to Erikson's stage theory?
What are the elements of the Cutter's identity? In other words, what makes a person a Cutter?

Why is there conflict between the Cutters and the Sochies (college stu-dents)? What does this conflict say about each group?

Dave's Dad says, "I was proud of my work. And the buildings went up. When they were finished the damnedest thing happened. It was like the buildings were too good for us. Nobody told us that. It just felt uncom-fortable, that's all." What does this tell us about how he is handling his life stage?

Attachment Theory

John Bowlby's (1958; 1969) seminal work on attachment theory, along with Mary Ainsworth's (1970) further delineation of attachment styles, provides a helpful framework to understand how early family experiences influence development and future relationships. It is very surprising how so many high school students find this theory fascinating and applicable to their lives and experiences. Most voraciously consumed the terms and ideas. Sometimes teaching revolves around providing the appropriate language for experience. Once the language is there, students have the means to examine, explore, apply, and synthesize.

Started by linking Attachment to what they recall of Erikson's infant stage (Trust v. Mistrust).

Attachment theory is similar in that it focuses on this earliest of relationships and what happens that is crucial to development. This theory provides a more in-depth look at how we might understand early life experience and how it may establish a style an individual may develop that has an impact throughout their life.

Explain the major concepts that Bowlby described in developing his theory of secure attachment. These include

Proximity Maintenance—The desire to be near the people we are attached to

Safe Haven—Returning to the attachment figure for comfort and safety in the face of a fear or threat

Secure Base—The attachment figure acts as a base of security from which the child can explore the surrounding environment

Separation Distress—Anxiety that occurs in the absence of the attachment figure

Show a video on Ainsworth's Strange Situation experiment to show the students how attachment styles can be identified in toddlers. There are

several available on YouTube such as that at https://m.youtube.com/watch?v
=QTsewNrHUHU. In addition to secure attachment, there are three types of
insecure attachment.

> *Secure Attachment*—Children who are securely attached do not experience
> significant distress when separated from caregivers. When frightened,
> these children will seek comfort from the parent or caregiver. Contact
> initiated by a parent is readily accepted by securely attached children
> and they greet the return of a parent with positive behavior.
> *Ambivalent Attachment*—Children who are ambivalently attached tend to
> be extremely suspicious of strangers. These children display consider-
> able distress when separated from a parent or caregiver, but do not
> seem reassured or comforted by the return of the parent. In some cases,
> the child might passively reject the parent by refusing comfort, or may
> openly display direct aggression toward the parent.
> *Avoidant Attachment*—Children with avoidant attachment styles tend to
> avoid parents and caregivers. This avoidance often becomes especially
> pronounced after a period of absence. These children might not reject
> attention from a parent, but neither do they seek out comfort or contact.
> Children with an avoidant attachment show no preference between a
> parent and a complete stranger.
> *Disorganized Attachment*—Children with a disorganized-insecure attach-
> ment style show a lack of clear attachment behavior. Their actions and
> responses to caregivers are often a mix of behaviors, including avoid-
> ance or resistance. These children are described as displaying dazed
> behavior, sometimes seeming either confused or apprehensive in the
> presence of a caregiver.

Have the youth apply their new understanding of Attachment to characters in
a story, *Ian and Cara*. Distribute the stories and questions ahead of the large
group discussion, so that students can think about and record their responses
before you discuss them as a class.

Ian and Cara

Ian and Cara met during college, finding much in each other. Ian found Cara
to be pretty, feminine, and rather shy. Ian charmed Cara and was able to entice
her to have sex with him on their second date. Cara was susceptible to his
charms because she doubted her desirability and was thrilled that a dominant,
charismatic man found her attractive. They lived together during their senior
years and married six months after graduation. They developed a traditional
relationship, with Cara staying home to mother their children while Ian

worked hard building his career. He was successful in his job, winning several lucrative promotions, but Cara began to feel that he was married more to his work than to her. She wanted him to talk to her more and do more things together. He wished that she was eating less and taking better care of herself.

What is Ian's attachment style? What evidence is there for this style?
What is Cara's attachment style? What evidence is there for this style?
How do their attachment styles affect their relationship?
In your opinion, what does the future hold for Ian and Cara?
How happy will they be with each other in another 10 years? Why?

Personal Reflection

Ask the youth to think of a story or incident they remember or heard about from their early childhood that involved them and a primary caretaker. For many, but not all people, that person was a parent. Ask them to write the story. After they complete it, ask them to identify the type of attachment that occurred for them during these years and explain their reasons why.

Suggest that they show their writing to the person in the story (or someone who knew about it if that person is not available). Get that reader's version of the story and see how similar (or different) it was from what they wrote. Ask the person to recall a different story about the early days of this relationship and write or record it for themselves.

Movie Application: Ordinary People

The film, *Ordinary People* (Redford, 1980), helps the students apply their learning about Attachment Theory to a film analysis. Briefly introduce the characters and encourage the class to think about Attachment theory as they watch the movie. Discuss it afterward.

What type of attachment style does Conrad have with his mother? Please explain your reasons.
What type of attachment style does Conrad have with his father? Please explain your reasons.
How do these attachments affect how Conrad deals with his brother's death?
When Conrad says, "I think I just figured something out . . . who it is who can't forgive who," what is he talking about?
What was it about the relationship that Conrad had with his therapist that allowed Conrad to gain insight about himself and begin to heal from

his depression? What did the therapist do that enabled Conrad to talk to him?

It may be easy to typecast the mother as cold and incapable of connection. What is a more compassionate understanding of what she is experiencing in the film?

What do you think makes this film resonate with so many people over time?

Movie Application: Forrest Gump

Introduce the characters and ask the youth to consider how attachment styles affect their relationships in *Forrest Gump* (Zemeckis, 1994). Use the following questions for the discussion.

What type of attachment style did Forrest have with his mother? What evidence does the film provide about this?

When in the film does Forrest make use of his mother as a safe haven?

How does Forrest's mother provide a secure base for him? Can you give an example that shows how this works for him?

How might you apply attachment theory to explain why the adult Forrest ran and ran and ran?

How did the attachment style that Forrest developed with his mother affect his relationships with Bubba? With Captain Dan?

What do you think Jennie's attachment style is? What are your reasons for identifying this style? How did Jennie's father affect her development?

How did the differences in their attachment styles affect Forrest and Jennie during their childhood years? In their young adult lives? Toward the end of their relationship together?

Jennie chooses to spend the end of her life with Forrest. What does that tell you about attachment?

Roles in the Family

The life stage and attachment theories can sometimes leave the impression that family influences solely determine the individual's development. Youth agency in the family might be ignored or undervalued. To balance this, engage them in a discussion about their roles in the family. This can also allow students living in two households to identify and compare the roles they assume in each setting and among different family constellations. For many, having an opportunity to examine their roles and hear from others from single or multiple family homes affirmed their circumstances in a unique and respectful way. Make sure that you clearly validate the variety of living situations that exist before beginning the discussion.

What family activities do you participate in?
What chores do you do?
How do you cooperate with members of your family?
What are family discussions like?
How do you show respect to other family members?
How do you show that you care about what happens to people in your family?
What say do you have in family decisions?
How do you help family members in need?
What makes you an important part of your family?

Chores Assignment

If you are a white, cisgender man, as is the author of this publication, you may recognize that you have many privileges. One of them is being able to present an activity like this without receiving a backlash that teachers who are less privileged might (and often do) get from doing things like this. That is a strong reason to get on it and use your privilege constructively.

The activity involves a homework assignment where students who identify as female do less work for the same grade than students who identify as male. Identities are those expressed by students at the start of the course. While this seemingly makes for a binary gender bias, greater inclusion might be worked on by describing the research and the assignment as such and discussing with the students how the assignment might be modified for those identifying as gender fluid or non-binary. When students so identify, talk to them about the activity beforehand and ask them how they would alter the activity for their participation.

Most students found the activity amusing upon first hearing it. Some challenged the underlying gender assumptions, while others affirmed it as accurate to their own lives. They reported that it provoked interesting discussions at home and a few parents at the school's open house voiced appreciation for someone else telling their children to do housework.

Explain the assignment to the youth.

There is research that shows that each teenage girl increases a mother's weekly housework by 1 ½ hours, but does not affect a father's typical housework time. A teenage boy, on the other hand, causes his mother to add three hours of extra work a week and about an hour to his father's time (Bianchi et al., 2000). *This would be the same for step-parents, and other adult guardians in the home.*

What do you think of these numbers?

What do you think it's like for the person who has the extra work?

What do you think they might rather be doing?

What would be a good thing to do about this? How can you help to change this?

In light of this data, your assignment, if you are male, is to do three hours of housework during school vacation week. If you are female, you must do 1 ½ hours of housework during school vacation week. Non-binary and gender fluid youth will consult with me about your hours. Have a parent or guardian write a brief report on what you did to send with you back to this class.

Thoughts on a Memoir

Anniversary, a short memoir written by Leah Truth (2007) provides students with a different lens for examining the family's impact on relationships. In this activity, students focus on how the author reflects on her parents' relationship as she navigates her own life. This models how an adult child can achieve agency even when such power was lacking in an earlier stage of life. The writer avoids simplifying her understanding of her parents' lives and it is an important lesson for students to realize that lives and relationships involve complexities. Students read the two-page essay and then discuss it with them.

Leah Truth writes about her parents on the day 45 years after they married. Why do you think she felt the need to write this story at this time?

What lessons about relationships did her parents teach her?

What conclusion does Leah come to about her parents?

What are your thoughts on how parent-child and sibling relationships in a family might affect a person's romantic relationship later in life?

To summarize, this topic grounds the study of relationships in the family, where first relationships are experienced. Important theories provide youth with background and vocabulary to understand how families influence an individual's development, including how they might influence future relationships.

Chapter 4

Friends

The examination of friendships includes looking at expectations and realities, good times and not-so-good times. Some common relationship themes are introduced here, with a closer look at how friendships affect romantic relationships occurring through future sessions.

Start with a meditation. Ring the chimes and guide their practice.

Sit comfortably with your back straight, with both feet on the floor. Close your eyes or look down to help block out distractions and focus on yourself and your own experience . . . Notice your breathing. Watch the air coming into and out of your body . . . Breathe in, breathe out.

I'm going to give you a prompt to use as you meditate. It's just one word. After you hear it, notice what comes into your awareness. Like a strip of words, images, memories, faces, places, like a scrolling at the bottom of a screen. Let the thoughts pass through. Try not to analyze what you see in your mind, just let whatever comes through be there, notice it, and let it pass to another thought or image. We'll do this for a few minutes.

Friendship.

After 2–3 minutes, bring them back slowly.

Bring your attention back to this room, where you are sitting.

Have the students pair up and talk about what they noticed during this meditation activity.

You choose what you want to tell your partner about your experience.

Refer back to the circle activity used in the discussion on Family to identify where they placed their friends in the circles.

How might closeness with a family member resemble closeness to a friend?

43

How might closeness with friends differ from that with family?
Why are friends especially important during adolescence?

THOUGHTS ABOUT FRIENDSHIPS

Distribute the *Thoughts about Friends* worksheet to give students an opportunity to reflect on these important connections. While they write their
responses to the questions for later discussion, play a variety of songs with
friendship themes.

Here are a few that youth suggested.

Bruno Mars—*Friendship Song* https://www.youtube.com/watch?v
=mGt3g6H4-kQ

Toy Story—*You've Got a Friend in Me* https://www.youtube.com/watch?v
=zIYOJ_hSs0o

Cher Lloyd—*Oath* https://www.youtube.com/watch?v=kpOY694Lwhs

Ben E. King—*Stand by Me* https://www.youtube.com/watch?v
=hwZNL7QVJjE

Bryant Oden—*Best Friends Forever* https://www.youtube.com/watch?v
=g9fBQYE-S5o

Lady Gaga—*You've Got a Friend* https://www.youtube.com/watch?v
=cAJPS_IC-A0

The purpose of the worksheet is to reflect on personal experiences, values,
and beliefs about friendships. The material generated in the worksheets brings
these thoughts to their awareness so that they will be more accessible to them
in the upcoming activities and discussions.

Thoughts about Friendship Worksheet

What do you like about your friends?

What are reasonable expectations of a friend? What do you think is okay
to ask of a friend?

What are some things that would not be fair to ask of a friend?

What strengths do your female friends bring to the friendship?

What strengths do your male friends bring to the friendship?

What strengths do your gender non-conforming friends bring to the friendship? (Gender non-conforming means that a person dresses, acts, has
interests and a sense of themselves that differs in varying degrees from
conventional or traditional norms for femininity and masculinity.)

What is unsatisfying about your female friends?

What is unsatisfying about your male friends?

What is unsatisfying about your gender non-conforming friends?
Besides gender, how else do your friends differ?
How do these differences affect your friendships?
Describe your ideal best friend.
What do *you* bring to your friendships?
What questions do you have about friendships as a topic?

Research studies on friendships show that people generally mention three main themes when it comes to characterizing their friendships (Miller & Perlman, 2009).

Caring and affection—friends know each other well and care for each other
Support and dependability—friends are reliable sources of comfort and help
Enjoyment and fun—friends take pleasure in each other's company

Do you see these themes appearing in your responses to the questions on the worksheet? How did you state them?

Distribute index cards and ask the students to write down the questions they wrote for #14 on a separate card for each question. Add some questions of your own. Place the cards on a table in the center of the room. Youth take turns picking up a question, reading it, and answering if they wish. The student reading the card goes first in responding to the question. Then any other students can add their response to the question or what was said about it. Facilitate for clarity, elaboration, or to expand their thinking.

A list of sample questions that students addressed in the sessions follows.

Why do people need friendships?
How are your friendships different now from when you were younger?
What five qualities do you value most in a friend?
Can pets be friends?
What factors affect the length of a friendship?
Some researchers find that one thing that characterizes friendships is that there is a lack of violence among friends. What are your thoughts on that?
What needs do friends fulfill that are not met by family members?
What are some problems that occur with friendships? (Record for later use)
What problem would you have the strongest reaction to?
What determines whether a friendship is worth saving?
Give an example of an injury that you think would allow a friendship to survive.

What injury would kill a friendship?
What do you think is a good way to end a friendship?
What is needed to maintain a friendship?

Expectations of Friendships

The preceding large group discussion will reveal much about the youths' understanding of friendship dynamics. Point out that this understanding can help them recognize that it is important to have expectations for these relationships. Divide them into small groups of four and assign them the task of specifying what these expectations would be. Compile a class list by consensus. Here is one of the lists created by students in the course.

TEXTBOX 4.1. FRIENDSHIP RULES

What rules do you have for your friendships?
- Volunteer help in time of need
- Trust and confide in each other
- Stand up for the other person in his or her absence
- Don't criticize each other in public
- Show emotional support
- Don't nag
- Engage in joking or teasing with the friend
- Seek to repay debts and favors and compliments
- Strive to make him or her happy while in each other's company
- Don't be jealous or critical of each other's relationships
- Share news of success with the other
- Ask for personal advice
- Disclose personal feelings or problems to the friend
- Be loyal; Never betray

Gossip

This is another topic that might be sensitive to some students so introduce it carefully with a reminder about the group agreements.

We're tackling this so that we can deepen our understanding of what gossiping is about. So let's start with this question, "What is gossip?"

After you discuss this a bit, add some ideas. Gossip occurs in conversations with friends. It involves talking about someone who is not there, usually about something that is not widely known. It is entertaining and frequently irresistible. Moral judgments are either stated explicitly or are implicitly understood by those involved in the conversation (McAndrew, 2008).

This warm-up activity comes from the *Telephone* game that many students are familiar with. Arrange them in rows, optimally six to a row. The first student gets a blank paper and pencil. Ask them to write the name of someone in the class at the top, and then fold it over to cover what they just wrote. They then pass the paper and pencil to the student behind them.

Ask the next student to write what happened last weekend (e.g., attended a concert, went bungee jumping, dressed up as _____). Have them fold the paper over to cover up what they wrote and pass it on the next student.

Ask the third student to complete the sentence stem "with _____" whom the preceding activity was done with, again using the name of another student in the class. Fold and pass again.

The next student writes where the activity happened (e.g., Skate Park, gym class, the town watchtower). Fold and pass behind to the next person again.

The fifth student writes the time when the activity took place (noon, midnight, 3:00 PM), folds it, and passes it on.

Ask the sixth student to write down the result of the activity (parents showed up, flat tire, found money), fold and pass it to the student in the row who wrote the first statement. This student reads the gossip story aloud.

Hopefully you get a laugh from the result and then discuss it.

How is gossip like the activity we just did?

How is it different?

On a scale of one to ten, with one being not an issue and ten being a major issue, where would you rank gossip as an issue for students at this school?

What are the reasons for your ranking?

Have you ever discovered that the gossip, a rumor, being spread wasn't true? What was that like?

Have you ever taken part in unwittingly spreading gossip, a rumor, that wasn't true? How did that happen?

What's wrong with gossiping?

Provide a link to a newspaper article (Carey, 2005) on gossiping for them to read and discuss: http://www.nytimes.com/learning/teachers/featured _articles/20050816tuesday.html

What was the previously held belief about gossip that the researchers mentioned in the article were trying to debunk?

Why might people find gossip "irresistible"?

How might gossip "sully (harm) reputations" in a group?

How might gossip offer "a foothold for newcomers" in a group?

How might gossip offer "a safety net" in a group?

What does it mean for gossip to be a "mutually protective ritual," according to the article?

How much of their daily conversation do people devote to gossip, according to the article?

To how many people is gossip usually passed by a single individual, according to the article?

How does gossip help "keep people from straying too far outside the group's rules"?

What was the conclusion of the experiment conducted by Dr. Wilson's team of researchers?

When does Dr. Wilson suggest that one "should gossip"?

What was the nature and conclusion of the experiment conducted by Dr. Kevin Kniffin?

How might "gossiping too little" be as risky as "gossiping too much"?

What is "social currency"?

How can gossip change a person's behavior "for the better"?

How might not participating in gossip be "unhealthy" or "abnormal," according to Dr. Wert?

What makes for an "adept" gossiper?

What purpose does gossip have in social media?

What effect does texting have on gossip?

Is gossip on-line different from harassment or cyber-bullying? If so, how?

How do you feel about having a gossip column in the school paper? The school's Facebook page?

Limits of Friendships

This activity explores the importance of placing limits on what a youth should do for a friend.

What would you do if a friend asked you for some money?

Seek their responses, adding variations like the amount of money ($5 or $50), the reasons for the request (get lunch or buy a gift for someone you don't like), or the history the friend has of not repaying loans. Discuss what conditions would prompt them to provide or refuse to give their friend money.

What are some things a friend might want to do that you might have to think about before responding?

Solicit 6–10 ideas and discuss them in small groups. Tell them to be sure to look at reasons for and against going along with a friend. Some ideas that emerged from previous groups included getting drunk, vandalizing school property, telling you a secret about someone, and cutting school or work to hang out and have fun.

After the small group discussions, talk in the large group.

What things would you NOT do for a friend?
What things would you ordinarily not do, but might do if a friend asked? Why?
What would you do for close friends but not other friends?
What did you notice about how you would limit what you would do for a friend?
How would this compare to what you would expect a friend to do for you?

When Friends Do More Harm than Good

This story from the *New York Times* (Duenwald, 2002) provides an interesting follow-up to the activity on friendship limits. It focuses on negative character- istics of friendships like betrayal, disrespect, illegal activities, and how such problems are dealt with. After giving the students the article to read https: //www.nytimes.com/2002/09/10/health/some-friends-indeed-do-more-harm -than-good.html discuss it as a large group.

Some of the issues raised in the article came up in our earlier discussions about friendships. What did the article add to your earlier perspectives?
What do you think determines the length of a friendship?
What do you think of Dr. Lerner's assertion about the lack of violence among friends? Do you agree with her? Why or why not?
What needs do friends fulfill today that may have been met by families and extended families in the past? Why do you think this is so?
What types of bad friends mentioned in the story seem most problematic to you? Which would you have the strongest reaction to?
Dr. Lerner says that what determines whether a friendship is worth saving "depends on how large the injury is." Can you give an example of an injury that you think would allow a friendship to survive?

What is an example of an injury that would result in the end of the friendship?
What do you think is a good way to end a friendship?

You can accompany this reading with a short video from the TED-Ed Student Talks (Hamric, 2019), where a 15-year old articulates how he experienced and eventually freed himself from a toxic friendship. After viewing it at https://www.youtube.com/watch?v=2pzZX33z-qE&utm_source=TED -Ed%20Subscribers&utm_campaign=259c2f09de2013_09_219_19_2013 _COPY_01&utm_medium=email&utm_term=0_1aaccced48-259c2f09de -47005505&mc_cid=259c2f09de&mc_eid=df6c446eab, ask for their reactions. Focus on feelings.

You realize that you have a really good friend. What feelings do you have about that?
You start to see a friend act like Leo Hamric's friend, Alex. This behavior continues. What feelings do you experience?
Like Leo, you end that toxic friendship. What feelings come to the fore?

Quotes about Friendships

Distribute this list of quotes about friendships for the youth to read. Ask them to code their responses to each statement on a Likert-type scale: SA for strongly agree; A for agree; U/N for uncertain or neutral; D for disagree, and SD for strongly disagree. In the discussion, have the students identify the statements they strongly agreed with and those they strongly disagreed with, and state their reasons.

Friendship Quotes

   "A friend is one who walks in when others walk out." Walter Winchell
   "A friend is someone who is there for you when he'd rather be someplace else." Len Wein
   "Everyone is a friend, until they prove otherwise." Anonymous
   "It takes a long time to grow an old friend." John Leonard
   "I get by with a little help from my friends." John Lennon
   "Friends are the Bacon Bits in the Salad Bowl of Life." Pizza Palace sign
   "Sometimes you pick your friends; sometimes they pick you." Anonymous
   "It's the friends you can call up at 4 A.M. that matter." Marlene Dietrick
   "I can trust my friends. These people force me to examine, encourage me to grow." Cher

"A new friendship is like an unripened fruit. It may become either an orange or a lemon." Anonymous

"Strangers are just friends waiting to happen." Anonymous

"Friends have all things in common." Plato

"The secret to friendship is being a good listener." Anonymous

"One loyal friend is worth ten thousand relatives." Euripides

"The only way to have a friend is to be one." Ralph Waldo Emerson

"Friends are those rare people who ask how you are and then wait to hear the answer." Anonymous

"A true friend is someone who thinks that you are a good egg even though he knows that you are slightly cracked." Bernard Meltzer

"Never kiss a friend. If you have deeper feelings, never reveal them. You will lose that friend forever." Anonymous

"Friends are born, not made." Henry Adams

"Life is partly what we make it and partly what is made by the friends whom we choose." Tehyi Hsieh

"If all my friends were to jump off a bridge, I wouldn't jump with them. I'd be at the bottom to catch them." Anonymous

"Friends are like pillars on a porch. Sometimes they hold you up and sometimes they lean on you." Anonymous

Be prepared to become immersed in the many issues that may come up with this discussion. Focus your facilitation on having the students respond to each other's comments so that the discussion moves mostly among them rather than a teacher-to-student dynamic.

Movie Application: *Whip it*

The film, *Whip It* (Barrymore, 2009), features a leading character that begins the film as an outsider at her school, but finds a way to break into a friendship circle. Watch the film, maybe invite the youth to bring popcorn to share. The post-film discussion revolved around these questions.

What are the clues that Bliss is an outsider at her school?

Corbi is friendly to Bliss at the pageant but quite different at the Oink Joint and later in the movie. What do you think are Corbi's motives for acting the way she did?

What does Bliss do to enter the Hurl Scouts?

What do the members of the Hurl Scouts do to "Let her in?"

What do you think of Bliss and Pasha's friendship?

What are the advantages and disadvantages of having friends around the same age?

What are the advantages and disadvantages of having older friends?

What are the advantages and disadvantages of having younger friends?

What do you think a friend should do when a partner of another friend acts like Oliver did?

How does homophobia affect male friendships?

What does Bliss get from her friends?

What does Bliss get from her family?

What was the most important characteristic of friendship displayed in the movie? Why do you think this is so important?

Movie Application: *Sisterhood of the Travelling Pants*

This film shows a group of four closely knit adolescent girlfriends trying to stay connected during a time apart (Kwapis, 2005). They do so by passing around a pair of old jeans that miraculously fits each one. They experience love, passion, grief, survival from abuse and neglect, disconnection, and reconnection.

How are each of the girls (Tibby, Carmen, Bridget, and Lena) outsiders in their worlds?

How did the girls differ from each other? Do the differences strengthen or weaken the friendships?

What do the pants do for the girls? What do the pants ultimately represent for them?

How does friendship save the lives of the four girls, either literally or metaphorically?

What lessons about friendship can we learn from the men and boys in the film?

What life lesson does each girl learn during the summer?

How does each change?

Loneliness

Involuntarily lacking friends can be very distressful for people at any age, but might be particularly difficult for adolescents for whom the peer group is so developmentally important. Some bonding among students has occurred by this time in your program, which is an important foundation before examining this sensitive topic.

What are some feelings that people might have when they're lonely?
What thoughts might occur?

Discuss factors that contribute to loneliness. Tell the students that some studies suggest that social and emotional isolation have causes (Weiss, 1973).

Social isolation is when a person doesn't have much opportunity to make connections because they don't have a social network of friends or acquaintances. They may live in an isolated area, for example, or don't belong to groups where connections occur. Can you think of circumstances that might create feelings of loneliness to people your age?

Emotional isolation happens when someone doesn't have a close intense connection with another person. They may lack a best friend.

How might this happen for someone your age?

Sometimes personality plays a part in loneliness.

What personality traits do you think might affect a person feeling lonely?
Without blaming someone for their own sense of loneliness, what skills might be lacking?
How might prejudice and discrimination foster loneliness?

As you begin to go deeper into the topic student responses can tend to reflect their own observations and experiences. In classes where you gauge that a high level of trust and safety exists, ask the students for their personal experience.

Raise your hands if you've ever felt lonely. What was that like?
How long did the feeling of loneliness last?
What made you feel stuck in it?
How did you come out of it?

We can regard loneliness as often being a temporary state. Ask the students to complete an assignment that might help reduce that time for others in the school. Divide them into groups of four, giving half of the class an assignment to make a poster addressing the question,

What are some ways to overcome loneliness?

Task the other half to create a poster answering the question, *What are some ways to help someone overcome loneliness?*

Hang the posters outside your meeting room or in heavily travelled areas of the building. Tell the youth to notice and report any conversations or reactions to the posters.

Topic Closure Activities

This topic covers a lot of ground, emotionally and content-wise. Giving students an opportunity to summarize what they got out of it or to highlight the kernels of insight most meaningful to them serves as a bridge to the coming study of romantic relationships. You can offer students a variety of options for accomplishing this.

Video Production

Using the TED Ed Student Talks video (Hamric, 2019) shown earlier as a model, student can use their cell phone or other devices to record a short 2–5 minute presentation on a friendship issue that was especially important to them.

Journal Entry

Encourage students throughout the course to keep a journal of their experiences. A journal entry can summarize the unit in a very personal way and by its nature can become a keepsake for review and reflection in the future.

Letter to a Friend

This option works like an entry into a gratitude journal. Students write a letter to a friend in their life, past or present.

Visual Artwork

Students can create a visual work of art depicting any concept about friendship that they choose. Many students take art classes in their schools and their choice sometimes addresses assignments in both courses. You and the art instructors may enjoy the cross-pollination and interdisciplinary nature of this work. For example, students' work from your group may appear in displays in the art wing.

Poems and Stories

Students could write their own works or find poetry or literature pertaining to friendships and write how that work affected them.

Music

While you will work with music in the context of the coming couple relationship units, you can also give students the opportunity to find and analyze a song about friendships. They may also write their own.

Chapter 5

Beliefs about Relationships

Begin focusing on romantic relationships by helping youth examine the beliefs they bring to the relationships they establish and experience. All of the students (and anyone teaching) come into the course with a set of beliefs about relationships. Aristotle's notion of the mind as a blank slate that is written upon as experiences accrue certainly does not apply by this time in youth's lives.

It is impossible not to have formed some ideas or thoughts based on experiences, observations, and the many influences they are exposed to, from families, friends, acquaintances, and the multitude of cultural messages they receive. They have beliefs about attraction, about how relationships begin, develop, and end, about how age, gender, sexual orientation, physical characteristics, personalities, personal histories, and countless other factors affect relationships.

In this section, you will investigate beliefs common to the cultures youth are familiar with. You will examine myths, comparing long held beliefs to research. As Academia does not hold exclusive rights to Truth, you will also see how the Arts portray beliefs about relationships.

BELIEF CARDS

This activity gauges student responses to 12 common beliefs about relationships (Bershad & Blaber, 1998). It engages students by soliciting their opinions about these beliefs and giving them opportunities to begin to state their own.

Divide the students into groups of four, giving each a pack of index cards on which you have written a belief statement on each card.

Opposites attract.

People lose their independence and individuality when they are in relationships.

In a relationship, you have to do what the other person wants.

Relationships work when people are committed and loving.

You must be in a relationship or you are nobody.

You have to work to make a relationship last.

If your partner doesn't know your wants and needs, they really don't care about you.

If you love someone, you need to show it.

Relationships are not forever.

Everyone has only one true love.

Relationships grow and change over time.

The best relationships involve mutual respect.

Place the pack face down. Have a student shuffle the cards and deal them to group members, who hide their cards from each other like a game of rummy. Students take turns reading a statement. The group tries to reach consensus about whether they fully agree, somewhat agree, somewhat disagree, or fully disagree with each statement. They sort the cards into piles for each position. If they cannot reach consensus, they place it in a mixed opinion pile. Encourage students to delve into each statement, explaining their views in detail and listening closely to others' views.

After each group completes their card piles, review each statement as a large group and determine if you can reach consensus as a class. In past practice, the only statements that students tended to reach a consensus on were their full disagreement with *"You must be in a relationship or you are nobody"* and full agreement with *"Relationships grow and change over time"* and *"Relationships work when people are committed and loving."*

As the curriculum suggests, you might give students a homework assignment to ask a friend or family member to identify their opinions on each statement, recording the reasons given. Encourage the students to converse with the person they interview, offering their own opinions as well. Caution students to carefully consider whom to ask.

Ask yourself if you are ready to hear a current partner's view.

What might be the pros and cons of asking someone?

Desired Dozen

This activity explores values and expectations of relationship partners. As you lead this popular activity be sure to occasionally remind the high schoolers to focus on their affective reactions to the task.

We are going to look at what you want in a partner in a romantic relationship. Think about what perspective you want to take as you participate in this activity. If you are single, pretend you are looking. If you are looking for a relationship, think about what you might want. If you are in a relationship, think of yourself as unattached for the purposes of this activity.

Ask the students to list six attributes they desire or want in a relationship partner. Have them consider personality and character traits, behaviors, emotional reactions, relational skills, physical features, and other factors.

When they finish their lists, arrange them in groups of three to discuss their six items. Ask them to explain their reasoning to each other. After about 5–7 minutes, ask them to add three more qualities to their list of what they desire or want in a partner.

Arrange for another set of small groups of three, making sure students are with people they haven't been with previously in the activity. Ask them to again discuss their lists and rationale. Have them add three more qualities to their own lists.

They now have a desired dozen on their lists. Ask them to rank order the qualities from most (1) to least important (12). Move back to your large circle to process the activity.

What did you notice about your thinking in deciding what to list?
How many of you have a perfect relationship with the desired dozen?
Is a perfect relationship possible?
Suppose you met someone who seemed to have all 12 qualities, but the longer you are with them, you discover they really don't. What if a missing quality was something in your top three expectations? How would that feel? What would you do?
How many qualities would you need to have a good relationship?
How did the other members of your groups affect your decision-making? Were they helpful or not?
How can you relate this activity to real life?
How might this compare to real life relationships?

Talk about having realistic expectations for a relationship, how one might initially think that the partner has "the desired dozen," but really doesn't, and that qualities might not be clearly seen in the initial "honeymoon" stage of the relationship. There may even be some unwanted qualities in the list that are not seen or not discovered until later. Discuss the role of friends and family members as influences on the relationship, beginning with how expectations are formed and selections made. Note how past relationships can prompt changes in expectations in future partnering.

Your concluding comments may be something like this.

> *You have a right to set expectations for a relationship partner and hopefully they are realistic. They reflect what you value in a relationship, what's important to you. You may not get all 12 cards and you may get some you would not have on your list, but being mindful of these expectations, these values, can keep you grounded, can help you evaluate how the relationship is going and how you want it to be.*

In another closing strategy for this activity, provide them with a list of qualities identified by American college students as their most important features of love (Fehr, 1988).

TEXTBOX 5.1. VALUES

- Concern for other's well-being
- Trust
- Caring
- Honesty
- Friendship

- Loyalty
- Commitment
- Acceptance
- Supportiveness
- Respect

How do these features compare with the values on your lists?

In some classes, you may need to give the students some additional help at the start. This may occur when there are many who have not yet experienced a romantic relationship or have some other difficulty identifying a desired dozen.

Characteristics of Healthy Relationships

An adapted activity from a domestic violence curriculum (Moles, 2001) offers another helpful strategy for identifying desirable and undesirable qualities in a partner. Provide them with a list of characteristics of a healthy and an unhealthy relationship. Ask students to check what they think are the three most important characteristics from the healthy list and the three most

TEXTBOX 5.2. CHARACTERISTICS OF HEALTHY RELATIONSHIPS

- Often have fun together
- Trust each other
- Make a commitment to be faithful
- Accept responsibility for their actions
- Are proud to be together
- Communicate about sexual touch
- Have equal decision-making power
- Apologize when wrong
- Maintain appropriate privacy
- Respect each other's opinions and abilities
- Support each other's goals and interests
- Get along with each other's friends and family
- Always feel safe with each other

TEXTBOX 5.3. CHARACTERISTICS OF UNHEALTHY RELATIONSHIPS

- Cheats or threatens to cheat
- Pressures the other for sex
- Doesn't listen
- Gets extremely jealous
- Puts the other down
- Threatens to leave or commit suicide
- Embarrasses or humiliates the partner
- Smashes, throws, or destroys things
- Goes back on promises
- Plays mind games
- Has ever grabbed, pushed, or hit the other
- Acts controlling and possessive
- Ignores the other

dangerous from the unhealthy list. Ask them to explain their ratings.

Alligator River

This classic exercise from the Values Clarification canon (Simon et al., 1972) consistently generates high engagement from youth. Here is an updated version of the story that changes some of the character names, notably changing Sinbad the Sailor to some other male name to deflect Islamophobia, and altering other details to make it more current. The activity has stood the test of time.

The characters are Abigail, Greg, Sam the Sailor, Janet (Abigail's mother), Julie (Abigail's best friend), Cherie', and Sluggo. Change any name that is the same as any student in the class. Set up the activity by asking students to listen to the story with a suspension of disbelief, as if they are watching a show where they know what is happening wasn't real, but they go along with it anyway. To add interest, draw the story on the white board as you tell it, listing the characters on the board.

Once upon a time there was a river that ran through a land far far away. People living on one side of the river had no means to cross it and they couldn't swim it because it was full of alligators. That's why they called it the Alligator River.

Abigail lived on one side of the river. Her boyfriend, Greg, lived on the other bank. They were so in love with each other and one day hoped to marry. They shouted across the river to each other but it only sharpened the pain of not being with each other in person. They didn't have a boat or a raft or the means to make one. Oh, how they pined to be with each other.

One day, Sam the Sailor came sailing up Alligator River on his trusty boat. He put in on the bank where Abigail lived. Abigail was ecstatic to see the boat. Now she had a way to get to Greg!

So Abigail approached Sam the sailor and explained what was going on and asked if he would sail her across the river to be with Greg. "Sure, no problem," he replied, "if you have sex with me."

Abigail was aghast! "What do you mean?" she sputtered.

"Have sex with me and I'll ferry you across the river. That's the deal," Sam said. "If you want some time to think about it, I'll be here until the tide changes tomorrow afternoon."

Abigail decided she needed some advice. She went to her mother, Janet, explained the situation and asked what she should do.

"I raised you to be an independent young woman," her mother told her. "You need to make your own decision about this."

"Ugh," thought Abigail, "that's no help." She next sought out her best friend, Julie.

After hearing the story, Julie responded, "What's the problem? Have sex with Sam and he'll take you over. Greg never has to know. It's no big deal."

Abigail thought and thought. She pondered. She listed pros and cons in her head. She agonized over the decision. Finally, out of her love for Greg, she chose to take Sam up on his offer.

Meanwhile, on the other side of the Alligator River, Greg was getting it on with Cherie'. He didn't tell Cherie' about Abigail. In fact, neither shared any sexual or relationship history with the other. Sluggo watched surreptitiously, looking for some advantage that might come his way. He hid in the bushes and spied on Greg and Cherie'.

True to his word, Sam took Abigail across the river the next morning. Abigail was overjoyed to see her beloved Greg. She jumped off the boat even before it anchored and ran to embrace Greg.

After a few joyous hours together, Abigail's conscience started bothering her. She firmly believed that their relationship required honesty. She felt compelled to tell Greg that she had sex with Sam in order to get across the river to see him.

"WHAT!" screamed Greg. "You whore! I can't believe you had sex with him!" He pushed Abigail away. "We're through."

Shocked and distraught, Abigail began to cry as Greg stalked off. Sluggo, who had been monitoring events from his hiding place up in a tree, came down and consoled Abigail. "Do you want me to go beat him up for you? Then I can come back and you can see how a real man treats his woman," he promised.

Abigail stared at Sluggo, unsure what to say.

The end.

Often students' immediate reactions included *"That's it?!" "What happened next?" "Really?" "What kind of a story is that?"*

After hearing their complaints smile and nod, and add a reminder that you told them to suspend their disbelief earlier, get to the meat of the activity, which is processing the story. Ask if there are any questions about the facts in the story. Then instruct them to rank order the characters from their most favorite (1) to least favorite (7). Request that they write down their rankings individually and to identify reasons for the rankings.

Next have them work in groups of four to discuss their rankings and determine if they can reach a consensus on the rankings. Give them about 15 minutes for this task. Rarely can a group reach consensus and then only if members "gave in," which, tell them, does not constitute consensus. Discuss the characters and story as a large group.

List the characters on the board. Ask for their rankings and list the numbers next to the names so that you can assess how the entire class viewed the characters. In this way, you can see who were the most and least favorite characters, although there will probably be significant variations. If you were to calculate the standard deviation, it would be large.

In past groups, many students reported that none of the characters was a favorite. All were disliked. Some students reported that their favorite characters were the alligators. But for the actual rankings, Cherie' usually came out as the most favorite, since students forgave her behavior because she was unaware that Greg was cheating on Abigail, so she was "innocent." Others were put off by her failure to communicate about sexual or relational history or because she was having sex without being married or in a relationship. Some questioned whether she was using safe sex or contraception.

Students tended to rate Greg as the least favorite, especially the female youth. Some male youth favored his ability to have two partners and "get away with it." When they voiced this opinion, the discussion sometimes became heated. In facilitating this, remind them of the group agreements and when necessary, push the boys' thinking.

Would you feel that way if Abigail was your favorite sister?

Usually this was not necessary as the girls could more than hold their own.

It may surprise you how high students (again mostly male) ranked Sluggo. His violence seemed to be an acceptable solution. Other students found him opportunistic and "sleazy."

Students had mixed opinions about Abigail. Some praised her "doing it for love" ethic. Some condemned her as naïve and lacking self-esteem, and even honor. Some students blamed her for being rejected by Greg. Female youth typically showed greater sympathy and viewed her character within the context of the story. They saw her prioritizing the relationship as a strength.

Students generally disdained the best friend as dishonest and unhelpful, and did not meet their criteria for being a "good friend." Many were more hostile toward the mother. They felt that she did not fulfill a mother's role in refusing to advise Abigail.

Sam the Sailor drew mixed opinions. Again, gender affected responses as the boys ranked him higher for his ability to obtain sex and his faithfulness in keeping his promise. Others (mostly girls) found him to be conniving and exploitive.

This is very much a capsule view of the discussions as many more opinions, observations, and insights came out of the discussions. In bringing the discussion to closure, make sure to address the following points.

What is the role of honesty in a relationship?
What is the relationship between emotional commitment and sexual intimacy?
When is sexual intimacy appropriate?
What double standard exists in what is expected for females and what is expected for males where sexuality is concerned?
Who gets rewarded?

Who gets punished? (This is especially important to discuss in groups
where Abigail's rating fell because she decided to have sex.)
*Where does this double standard come from? How does it affect people?
How have you observed it operating?*
What is the role of a parent in this situation?
What is the role of a friend?
What traits do the characters possess?
What values do they represent?

TEXTBOX 5.4. VALUES ISSUES
IN ALLIGATOR RIVER

- The role of honesty in a relationship
- The relationship between emotional commitment and sexual intercourse
- Exploitation in a personal relationship
- Appropriateness of sexual intercourse
- Role of a friend
- Role of a parent
- The double standard
- The meaning of engagement
- Honoring a contract
- Resolution of conflict
- Revenge
- Misogyny (blaming a woman for the circumstance)
- Disclosing (or seeking) relevant information
- Selfishness
- Opportunism
- Sacrificing for love

This last question gets to the primary objective of the activity—to help students see that the rankings of the characters and the characters themselves represent relationship values that are important to examine. Post the following list for them to consider and discuss.

This is the point of the story.

Do the rankings you gave to the Alligator River characters actually reflect your own personal values about relationships?

Articles of Love and Relationships

There is value in using a variety of teaching methodologies so that youth may experience different approaches in examining relationship topics. Experiential learning, where teachers present activities that embody the concepts being taught, can be particularly effective. Expand your investigation of relationship beliefs with this concrete "show-and-tell" experience. Assign students to bring in an object that represents some value, belief, or message about love or relationships.

This activity may not be a good idea for Valentine's Day. There are students whose experience of the holiday is marked with sad memories of break-ups and rejections. The assignment can swerve to highlight those memories and result in feelings of sadness and regret

Discourage them from bringing in rings and other jewelry. These objects tend to be over-represented in the collection. Too many bring in jewelry that their partners gave them and this lack of variety can make for a boring exposition.

Remind the students a few times before the assignment is due. Having the day arrive with only a few students completing the assignment makes for a very brief activity. Here is a sample reminder.

> *Don't forget to bring in your object (and brunch treat) on Friday!*
> *It might be a work of art, an object, a brief writing such as a poem or short letter, a keepsake or whatever else comes to mind. Please try not to bring a picture of a loved one or the traditional ring/necklace/bracelet.*
> *S-T-R-E-T-C-H your thinking on this.*
> *You will bring this object to class on Friday and explain its significance to the class.*

Introduce the session with a brief look at multicultural experiences, including signs and symbols of love and relationships. Showing images on a PowerPoint of a variety of couples. Some ideas would be a wife and husband from India, Ellen DeGeneres and Portia de Rossi as an example of lesbian and celebrity culture, a sub-Saharan African husband and wife, an orthodox Jewish couple from Brooklyn, gay men, an older couple wearing green at a St. Patrick's Day gala, and Beyoncé and Jay Z.

> *What do you know about how different cultures value and experience romantic relationships?*
> *What other images from different cultures come to mind?*
> *What can looking at cross-cultural influences on relationships teach us?*

The show-and-tell phase of the session involves having students voluntarily show what they brought to class and explain its significance. Have the youth listen without comment.

A vast majority of students took this assignment quite seriously, as evidenced by their artifacts and explanations. There were baby blankets, musical instruments, vacation memorabilia, athletic gear, paintings, drawings, sculptures, dishes, tools, and many, many photographs. They talked about a parent dying of cancer, a grandmother's cooking, a boyfriend's kindness, a girlfriend's courage, and about being accepted as a trans-youth. There can be many stories touching the heart. Some stories that in other contexts might be seen as mundane have their own special poignancy from being shared in this space. While not every class has this magic, most of them do.

Thank each participant after their presentation and thank the entire class after the last one. Present your own artifact to participate in the ever-developing relationship you are having with these youth.

Problematic Beliefs

Adolescents are working on formulating their beliefs and opinions, including how they think about and view these very concepts. Many tend to give others a great deal of space, perhaps even leniency, in an effort to show respect for others' beliefs. This can make disagreeing with someone's belief difficult and can severely hamper critical thinking. You need to challenge them to find ways to show respect for people, but to think critically about people's beliefs. You can help them learn to maintain civility when pointing out faulty reasoning. Start this discussion by asking them:

Are all beliefs valid?
Are all beliefs worthy of respect?
Some people used to believe the earth was flat (apparently some still do).
   Do you respect that belief?

After this initial discussion, show them a list of problematic beliefs for evaluation.
Common Problematic Beliefs about Relationships

Being in a relationship will meet all my needs.
Partners are responsible for each other's feelings. For example, if one
   partner is unhappy, it's the other one's fault.
A disagreement is a sign that the relationship is falling apart.
A good relationship is always exciting, romantic, and fun.
I can't be a whole person if I'm not in a relationship.

Partners don't have to compromise if they are in a good relationship.
Partners should always tell each other everything.
You can change a partner who has flaws.
If a relationship isn't perfect, it's time to leave.

Have the students read the list and write notes about their reactions to each statement. They can refer to their notes as you discuss the list together.

What statements do you see as dysfunctional?
What beliefs do you agree with?
Select a statement that you think is clearly dysfunctional. What's wrong with it?
Are you saying that a belief may be wrong?
How do you think these beliefs might harm a person in a relationship?
Select a belief that you think might cause problems in the relationship. Why do you see it that way?
Can you think of other beliefs that might work against building a healthy relationship?

Soul Mates: Reality or Myth?

Students are not immune to the effects of romantic comedies, including the common theme that a special someone exists somewhere out there for each person. As one student remarked, "Everyone has a soul mate." To explore this issue, distribute two articles (Meyers, 2007; Solomon, 2019) for students to read individually. Divide them into groups of four and assign the groups to write a summary of each article and create three questions on each for class discussion.

Some of the questions they wrote included:

Do you believe in soul mates? Why or why not?
How can the idea of needing to find a soul mate work against you?
Can there be positive things about having or wanting to have a soul mate?
Have you heard of real life stories of people who have found their soul mates?

Movie Application: Riding in Cars with Boys

The reality of relationship experiences often does not conform to the beliefs people grow up hearing about from parents, family, television shows, and

movies. The happily-ever-after theme echoed in countless romantic comedies, adventure tales, and novels can occur in some real life relationships, but
also include pain and sorrow, breakups and endings. Even those most likely
to be seen as healthy relationships have periods of problems and difficulties.
Helping students develop a more nuanced view of relationships brings many
cultural beliefs into question.

Riding in Cars with Boys (Marshall, 2001) offers such a view. The main
character, Beverly, finds her beliefs and expectations shattered by reality. She
suffers, endures, and comes out strong. The film also helps students examine
how the parent-child relationship across generations influences and interacts
with romantic relationships.

Watch the film and discuss the following questions.

> *As a child, what did Beverly learn about boys and relationships from her friends?*
> *What beliefs about relationships didn't work out for Beverly as a teenager?*
> *What belief about relationships of your own was supported in the film?*
> *What belief do you hold about relationships that was challenged or not supported in the film?*
> *What beliefs about a parent-child relationship are portrayed in the film?*

Conclude the discussion by asking:

> *What is a belief about relationships that you have that was not presented in the film?*

Movie Application: Imagine Me & You

This film (Parker, 2005) presents sexual orientation as a factor in the
love-at-first-sight theme in the romantic comedy genre.

> *What beliefs about relationships can you identify in the film?*
> *Would you consider the relationship beliefs in this movie more aligned with the partner as destined soul mate or partner has to work to make a relationship work belief set? What examples can you cite?*
> *What is a belief presented in the film that you disagree with? Why?*
> *How does homophobia affect the relationship?*
> *What do you think about how Heck, Rachel's husband, dealt with Rachel's falling in love with Luce?*
> *What did you think of Coop's behavior toward Luce?*
> *Will Rachel and Luce live happily ever after?*

In summary, examining beliefs about relationships introduces a cognitive aspect that gives youth an opportunity to examine their own thoughts and to hear the perspectives of their peers in the group. Allowing them to also scrutinize cultural beliefs about relationships gives them a broader context in which to reflect upon the expectations and values they might bring to their actual relational experiences.

Chapter 6

Relationship Theories

An important value to transmit to youth involves helping them learn and use scientific thinking and critical analysis in regard to relationships. High school students are capable of the deeper thinking required to comprehend how theories are built, supported, altered, or rejected. Studying theories hones their ability to reason and reflect and provides tools for identifying and combatting bias. This part of the course examines the science of relationships, using theories developed from research that incorporates the scientific method and conceptual thinking.

> *Theories are ways of explaining things. They try to answer the questions why and how. What is a theory you can name?*
> *Theories can sometimes be difficult to understand, but sometimes even a young child can get the basics of a theory. For example, here's how to teach first graders about Einstein's Theory of Relativity.*

Draw on the whiteboard a series of fish swimming in different directions. Have some swimming up, some down, some left, some right, some diagonally.

> *Who's winning the race?*

The children understood that it depends on which way you are going to which finish line and that it could be any direction. In other words, they understood that it's all relative.

> *We will examine different theories and see if they complement or contradict each other. Our goal is to deepen our understanding of relationships.*

In this section you will guide their examination of theories by didactic presentations, or articles, experiential activities, instruments used to validate scales or measure variables integral to the theories, discussions, and film reviews. To incorporate their own rich perspectives, assign them to bring in a song and lead a class discussion analyzing the lyrics and music. Be sure to include references to the major theorists in the discussions. Youth rated this activity highly in their course evaluations. See the earlier explanation of this activity in chapter 2.

Examining Rubin's Love Scale

Rubin's (1970) was an early effort to try to empirically measure love. Having a historical perspective fortified the understanding that science starts with an idea, broadens that idea into related concepts, and explains how these concepts build from the beginning idea. An early theory can be built upon, by adding new ideas or rejecting older ones. Then the new theory is presented and it is challenged. Science is not a static, once and done effort. Rubin's theory may be your starting point, but it will not be where you end up, nor will the last theory you study be the last word.

Rubin's Love Scale postulated that love encompasses three aspects:
Intimacy—I feel that I can confide in my partner about virtually anything.
Dependence—If I could never be with my partner, I would be miserable.
Caring—I would do almost anything for my partner.

This theory presents love as a multifaceted experience that involves both giving and taking. Distribute Rubin's Love Scale for the students to complete either as themselves or by adopting a different persona for their responses. The purpose is to investigate the theory, using the scale as a representation of the ideas. The instrument directs participants to report their answers on a 9-point Likert-type scale from *Not True (1)* to *Definitely True (9).*

Sample items include:
If [loved one] were feeling badly, my first duty would be to cheer him/her up.
  I feel that I can confide in [loved one] about virtually everything.
  If I could never be with [loved one], I would feel miserable.

After taking the survey, address these questions:

Can you identify which items addressed each of the three components of
  Rubin's theory?
How well did you think the statements captured these components?
What is your opinion of Rubin's theory? Would you add anything? Delete
  anything?

What might be another way of testing Rubin's theory besides this paper survey?

The Johari Window

The Johari Window proposes that relationship growth or contraction depends on the quality and quantity of information one has about a partner and oneself (Luft & Ingham, 1955). It uses four "window" panes to describe this concept (see figure 6.1).

The four panes show four dimensions of information giving and receiving. The two on the left (Open and Hidden or Secret) are visible and known to you. The two on the right are unknown to you. People see themselves clearly when they share the left two and are open to learning from the two on the right.

OPEN: Also called the public area, this pane is visible to you and to other people. It includes your appearance and what you tell others about yourself.

When you first came into this classroom, it was open to me that you were students and open to you that I was the teacher. When we shared names and pronouns, we expanded our open areas to each other.

HIDDEN: This window is only visible to the individual. It may be things you haven't told others yet or things you may choose to keep secret. Depending on what the information is and who you are with, you may be very cautious and perhaps never reveal this information. This might involve fears, resentments, weaknesses, or past experiences. You need to trust the other, to feel safe, in order to expand this area. Some information, like a favorite color or dessert, holds little threat and you may disclose easily. The nature of the disclosure will determine how much you shrink the *Hidden* pane, which automatically enlarges the *Open* pane. Doing so can help you build a relationship if the information you disclose is heard and you feel respected. This is what builds trust. If the information you disclose is poorly received, you may tend to withhold similar information from this person in the future.

OPEN	BLIND
HIDDEN	UNKNOWN

Figure 6.1. Johari Window

BLIND is the pane where others have information about you that you are not aware of. Sometimes this might be your facial expressions or body language. You may exhibit tension that you are not aware of but that others can see or hear in the tone of voice you use or your posture. When people tell you what they notice, it decreases your *Blind* area and enlarges your known *Open* area.

> *When I travel in another country, I often become aware of my larger blind area whenever I get looks from people there that I do not know how to interpret. I find that as a white cisgender man, that I am blind to many of the experiences of folks who are marginalized because of race, gender, ethnicity, and other factors. I need to work on this area to better understand others' experiences and perspectives.*

UNKNOWN is what is invisible to you and to others. It might be about an experience you haven't had or something in your subconscious. It might be a feeling related to a past experience that you haven't yet understood or connected. As you get closer to people and engage in a process of listening and disclosing respectfully and honestly, you increase the possibility that your unknown area will shrink and your self-knowledge expand.

Discussion:

> *What information is quickly conveyed into the Open area when you first meet a person?*
> *What information from our Hidden area would be easy to disclose in the early stages of a relationship?*
> *What information might take a while to share?*
> *What are some things that someone might have in their blind area?*
> *What is something in a person's Hidden area that they might like to change?*
> *What experiences might promote discovery of information in the Unknown pane?*
> *The Johari Window can be a useful tool in monitoring the status of a relationship. Are Open areas expanding? Are the other areas shrinking? What happens to affect the size of the panes?*

Sternberg's Triangular Theory of Love

Sternberg (1987) postulated three core elements of love that are different from Rubin's formulation. While intimacy, passion, and commitment formed Sternberg's three bases, his theory allowed for a total of seven different types of love (and possibly an eighth, non-love). He achieved this by blending the three core elements, the points of the triangle and making the blending of all three the highest form of love.

Sternberg defined his three core elements as:
Intimacy—feelings of warmth, understanding, communication, support, and sharing
Passion—emotional arousal and sexual desire
Commitment—the decision to stay in a relationship and to work to maintain it.
Show them a YouTube video presentation providing an explanation of the theory https://www.youtube.com/watch?v=-Cxq7ZmnFLU.
Discuss the following questions.

What are your thoughts on this theory?
Which aspects are most important to you?
Rubin had Caring as a core element in his theory. Where would caring belong in Sternberg's?
Do you think that people in relationships experience these components at the same time or do you think there are changes over time?
High levels of passion do not last. How does Sternberg's theory accommodate that reality?
Of Passion, Intimacy, and Commitment, which do you think people have the most control over? The least control over?
Do you think people's actual experience of relationships fall neatly into these types?

Romantic, Passionate Love

Helping teenagers gain understanding on the role that emotions play in relationships is a complex task on many levels. The Feeling Thermometer (see figure 04.01) provides a basic tool to bring awareness to present emotional states. Zillmann's (1984) ideas explain about how emotional arousal contributes to the start of relationships and affects subsequent events as well.

Zillmann proposed that romantic love involves passion and that *any* form of strong arousal, pleasant or unpleasant, can influence feelings of romantic love. *Excitation transfer* occurs when arousal caused by one event fuels stronger emotional reactions to a second, unrelated event. When experiencing a strong emotion in a context, like when hearing a highly charged song on a crowded dance floor, that emotion can be transferred to a secondary event in the same context. Eyes meet across the dance floor and that interaction gets similarly charged. This event fits Zillmann's notion that the person across the floor is thought to be the cause of the arousal. His research showed that men were more influenced by this process than women.

The concept for students to examine is that emotional arousal from a different source, whether positive or negative, can fuel the intensity of emotions in a relationship. These emotions, furthermore, can affect thoughts and perceptions. Ask students to provide examples of this. Here are some insights youth shared.

> *Getting a bad test grade and coming into the hall and seeing a partner talking with someone else. They're flirting!*
> *Having a heated argument and then making up and making out.*
> *Going on a fast ride in an amusement park and getting physically close after getting off.*
> *Getting in an intense workout at the gym and feeling attracted to someone doing the same thing.*

Since the theory proposed that one's thoughts can be influenced by emotions, go a little further and ask them:

> *How does a person understand that these emotion-driven thoughts might not be helpful, that decisions made during these times might not be what we might make otherwise?*

In most classes, students got the point and suggested pausing, talking to a trusted friend to get a "reality check," identifying the feelings (the feeling thermometer again), going with the feeling only up to a point, and taking a bathroom or other break to gather one's thoughts.

Lee's Styles of Loving

Lee (1998) identified six styles of love, using Greek terms as names for each type. Describe each style, using PowerPoint or notes written on the board. Ask students to copy the definitions in their notebooks so they can reference them for later work (and quizzes). You could utilize a website that explains Lee's theory using brief clips for television and film productions (https://www.theodysseyonline.com/six-styles-of-love-in-popular-culture).

Lee's styles are summarized as follows.

The *Eros* style emphasizes passionate, romantic love, with a focus on physical beauty and pleasure. People with this style tend to engage in "love at first sight" and are quickly swept away with the sensual/sexual aspect of the relationship. Sex can happen pretty quickly in the relationship. Being affectionate and erotic are characteristic behaviors. A more attractive potential partner can lure *Eros* away.

Ludus values fun and play with little or no commitment. Seduction and sexual conquest occur, with little or no commitment. Relationships are for fun; tend to be casual, and brief. Having many partners, sometimes simultaneously, happens because *Ludus* enjoys people. Getting too serious scares a *Ludus* away.

Mania takes the partner on an emotional roller-coaster ride. This style demonstrates possessiveness and can become intensely jealous. The Manic style thrives on emotional intensity, often manufacturing turmoil. They are deeply, ecstatically in love, but can become painfully agitated at the smallest perceived slight.

Storge (STOR-gay) represents companionship. Slow to develop the sensual or sexual experience and commitment, but tends to endure as it progresses. This style may grow a friendship into a relationship, and focuses on open and deep communication, mutual concern, and a peaceful and calm way of relating to the partner.

Pragma brings a practical style to a relationship. Sharing commonalities, being in the same class, neighborhood, having similar interests and emphasizing mutual satisfaction characterize *Pragma*. This style values rational thinking, often engages the partner in mutual and equitable decision-making, and greatly values compatibility.

The *Agape* style represents a selfless kind of love, where the partner's satisfaction and well-being is more important than one's own. There is caring and giving without expecting reciprocation. They may idealize the partner and are never demanding.

After the presentation of the styles, discuss them.

> *Without mentioning any names, which styles do you observe present at this school?*
> *Why do you think these styles exist here among your classmates?*
> *What style might make the best relationship? The worst?*
> *Which styles would match best?*
> *Which styles would be a terrible match?*
> *How might a person develop a particular style?*
> *Do you think a person's style might change? If so, what could cause this?*
> *Can you think of a fictional character (television, movies, or book) that fits a particular style?*

As a follow-up to the discussion, assign students to work in pairs to develop a scenario depicting a scene from a relationship between people with two of the styles (they could be the same style). Have the students act out their scenario and challenge the rest of the class to identify what they portrayed.

An alternative follow-up is to ask students to write a story of a couple in a relationship. They are to pick a style from Lee's theory for each partner in their stories.

> *Don't identify the name of the style, but include the characteristics of that style.*
> *Write how they began, how they established connection, how they experienced connection, and then disconnection happens, like a problem in the relationship. Leave your ending unresolved.*

They then exchange stories and work to identify the styles of the partners. Ask them to decide whether reconnection would or should happen and discuss the reasons why and why not. Finally, if they decide that reconnection was possible and desired, they are to finish the story describing how reconnection occurred.

Sumerlin's Relationship Stages

John Sumerlin's (1979) dissertation on relationships provides an intriguing theory for youth to examine. His work proposes a five-stage theory of relationships to explain to the youth.

Contact heralds the start of a relationship and is most often spurred by physical attraction. It is a time when hopes and dreams for a relationship are projected onto a prospective partner. It is thus a romantic, fantasy-based time. "It is as if we have always known each other," is a representative comment. The partner is idealized, desirable, and good qualities are seen and emphasized, and negative ones unseen or disregarded.

Partners at this stage focus on their positive qualities and commonalities and seem to be trying to merge their identities. They might often talk about how similar they are. Emotions are highly charged during this phase. Partners can't wait to see each other. Sexual feelings can further compound the illusion, feeding euphoria and increasing the intensity. A person at this stage might report that "We are always touching."

> *What do you think about how Sumerlin characterizes this stage?*
> *What have you observed happening at the start of a relationship?*

Confrontation occurs when the bubble bursts and the person discovers that the partner is not perfect. Dreams are shattered as reality sets in. There can be agitation, anger, pain, and disillusionment. They may ask, "Hey, what's going on? You're not the person I thought you were." Maybe they were on their best behavior during the *Contact* stage but couldn't keep the effort going. Most relationships end at this stage, sometimes quite abruptly.

> *How does this sound to you?*
> *How long do you think it takes for this stage to come after the Contact stage?*
> *What are some things that might prompt Confrontation?*

Depression is the third stage and occurs when partners emerge from the Confrontation phase and decide to continue. Despite discovering that the relationship isn't perfect and that there are things that need to be worked out, there is a commitment to undertake what is necessary to keep things going. They may say things like "So my partner isn't perfect; this is still the best relationship I've ever had and if we work at things, well, they might get better." Feelings of loss about the fantasy of what the relationship was and the dreams related to that fantasy may be present. Guilt may play a role in this stage too, as a partner might think that it is their fault if a breakup occurs.

> *What do you think about this stage?* (Many students reported that this theory was starting to make *them* feel depressed).
> *What may make people decide to continue a relationship despite seeing its flaws?*

Dissociation, the fourth stage, focuses on maintaining a stable relationship. In effect, the relationship becomes more important than individual personal satisfaction. Uncomfortable emotional material may be withheld (as explored earlier in *The Johari Hidden Window*). There may be fear that such disclosure will turn into more problems and threaten the relationship. They may think that a break up might occur if they were honest about some things. There is less spontaneity in this stage, less candid sharing and less freedom and comfort due to the need to put energy into controlling what is said and done. Some relationships never progress beyond this stage.

> *What do you think about this stage?* (Now some students may moan that they are *really* depressed).
> *How might a couple remain stuck in this stage? What might cause this?*

Integration happens when partners look to facilitate and support each other's individual growth even if that development might drive them apart. For example, they may support a partner's decision to go to college far away because that is the best place to study what they are interested in.

Uncomfortable material is shared and worked on with partners nurturing each other, listening to understand each other's perspectives. Real intimacy occurs. This greater risk-taking to support personal development may end the relationship or make it stronger.

> *What do you think of this stage?*
> *Sharing what kinds of uncomfortable emotional material might serve to end the relationship?*
> *What kind might strengthen it?*
> *What might a breakup at this stage look like?*
> *What do you think of this theory now that you've heard about all of the stages?*

Since this is the final theory you will examine, ask the students to review their notes about each theory, in preparation for a summary discussion.

> *Which theory or theories do you think best explains relationships?* (Interestingly, college students typically chose Sumerlin's theory. High school students varied in their opinions. None stood out as dramatically more preferred than the others.)

Movie Application: Reality Bites

This movie (Stiller, 1994) tells about a group of post-college friends in the 1990s who deal with the complexities of entering young adulthood, or what psychologists today refer to as emerging adulthood. Viewers witness close friendships providing support, challenge, and the potential for romantic relationship. The experiences with two potential partners come to the fore as well. There is much in the film to investigate using the theories.

Watch the film and discuss the following questions. It's helpful to show the questions and allow time for students to make notes on the items before the discussion.

> *Rate the following characters in the order of whom you liked best and identify your reasons. (Lainie, Troy, Vickie, Sammy, Michael)*
> *Think about Lee's Styles of Loving. What types did you see present in the characters in the movie?*
> *Vickie said, "Sex is the quickest way to ruin a relationship." Do you agree or disagree?*
> *How can Sumerlin's relationship stages be applied to Lainie and Troy's relationship?*

Which qualities were shown by what characters?

Movie Application: Perks of Being a Wallflower

Highly regarded by professionals in the mental health field, this movie (Chbosky, 2012) respectfully addresses mental illness and trauma in the context of adolescent friendships and relationships. The main characters, Charlie, Sam, Patrick, Brad, Mary Elizabeth, and Craig provide interesting character studies, more so in their relationships with each other. The experience of gay youth is sensitively portrayed here as well.

> *Using Lee's theory, identify what type of love Charlie had for Sam. Give reasons to support your answer.*
>
> *Using Sternberg's theory, identify the type of love Charlie had for Mary Elizabeth. Give reasons to support your answer.*
>
> *Considering the Johari Window, explain why Brad did not shrink his hidden area (regarding his relationship with Patrick) to his friends.*
>
> *Thinking of Sumerlin's stages, what happened in the confrontation stage between Sam and Craig?*
>
> *What was revealed about Charlie's unknown area near the end of the film?*

To further explore the issues in the movie, ask the students to use any of the theories discussed in class to write a paper providing a detailed analysis of any of the relationships in the movie.

Movie Application: Student Choice

As further follow-up, give students the choice of selecting any movie about a romantic relationship that they wished to analyze. Have their paper address the following.

> *Rate the characters in the order of whom you liked best and identify your reasons.*
>
> *Think about Lee's Styles of Loving. What types did you see present in the characters in the movie?*
>
> *How was Sternberg's theory demonstrated by the characters?*
>
> *How can Sumerlin's relationship stages be applied to the relationship(s)?*
>
> *Which qualities were shown by what characters?*

To summarize, challenging youth to examine theories about relationships bolsters their critical thinking skills and opens another avenue from which to view relationship issues. As they encounter a variety of frameworks from which to analyze relationships, they can develop a repertoire to use in their own relational experiences.

Chapter 7

Starting a Relationship

"I've never been in a relationship. How do you get started?"

This student's question prompted the creation of this section of the program. You might follow this with a literature review of how others addressed this question. For example, studies of American and Canadian couples show that two out of three couples today started out as friends, with the percentage even higher for LGBTQ+ couples (Stinson et al., 2021).

But there are already experts to tap in your classroom.

After the opening meditation and feeling thermometer check-in, distribute a blank paper to each student and ask them to write, anonymously, their answer to the question:

What do you tend to notice first when you see a person for the first time?

When they finish, tell them to roll the paper up into a ball and throw it into the center of the room.

Get a paper that is not your own.

Write the sentence stem *"This person wrote . . ."* on the white board and ask them to follow the phrase with what was written on the paper they picked up. Then discuss it.

What did you notice about the statements?
What themes emerged?
Why do you think appearance is so much at the forefront of people's minds?
What judgments are we making at the outset?
How accurate are these judgments?
Why do you think we make such judgments in the first place?

Note that you began taking a glimpse at starting a relationship in the theory unit. Ask what they remember of this. They usually refer to Sumerlin's *Contact Stage* and how Lee's *Styles of Loving* gave some inkling about what people looked for. Tell them you will go a bit deeper into the start of a relationship.

Divide the students into groups of three or four and assign them to write a one-page story about how a relationship starts for people their age. They can use names of youth that are not in this school but are to avoid any racialized or other stereotypes. Tell them the stories will be read to the class.

Process the stories like you did with the sentence stems, noting themes and judgments. Discuss how realistic each story seems. Ask them to predict the future of each relationship.

First Impressions

Select a picture of a group of youth similar in age and appearance to your group from a public domain source. Show it on a projector screen to start the discussion.

> *What are your first impressions of these people?*
> *How fast did you start making judgments of them?*

According to researchers (Bar et al., 2006), participants in a study took 39 milliseconds (1/25th of a second) to determine if a person's face looked angry. It took longer (one-tenth of a second) to judge ability, trustworthiness, competence, and aggressiveness (Willis & Todorov, 2006). It took a whopping five seconds to determine how extraverted, conscientious, and intelligent the person was (Carney et al., 2007).

> *What do you think about these research results?*
> *Why do you think these impressions occur so quickly?*
> *What have you noticed about how you experience first impressions of others?*
> *What have you noticed about people's first impressions of you?*
> *How much do you think first impressions matter?*

Researchers (Sunnafrank & Ramirez, 2004) conducted an experiment where they arranged a get-acquainted activity involving conversations among new classmates. They solicited first impressions and found that these initial judgments influenced students' feelings about each other nine weeks later in the course.

Present an activity to address the accuracy of first impressions.

Take a moment to form a quick judgment of someone who is—resentful,
  stubborn, nit-picking, impulsive, hard-working, and intelligent.
Would you want this person as a co-worker? (Youth often responded
  "Probably not!")
Now, consider someone who is intelligent, hard-working, impulsive,
  nit-picking, stubborn, and resentful.
Would you rather have him or her as a co-worker than the first one?

Both descriptions contain the same qualities, but are listed in a different
order. This illustrates what psychologists call the primacy effect—a tendency
for the first information received about others to carry special weight.

Which then leads us to ask, how accurate are our first impressions?
What do you think these impressions are being based on? (Mention stereotypes if the students don't.)

Darley and Gross (1983) found that biases and stereotypes are at work
when people form their first impressions. The researchers showed college
students a video of a fourth-grade girl, whom they named Hannah. Dividing
the college students into two groups, they told one group that Hannah came
from a wealthy background and told the other group she came from a less
advantaged status. The researchers gave no information about Hannah's academic abilities.

They then showed one group a short video of Hannah playing in a plain
fenced-in school yard. Her neighborhood was in a city with run-down homes.
The school she attended was depicted as a "three-story brick structure set
close to the street, with an adjacent asphalt school yard" (Darley & Gross,
1983, p. 23). They reported that Hannah's father was a meat-packer and her
mother a seamstress working at home.

The researcher showed another group of students a different video of
Hannah playing in a park lined with trees. This neighborhood was in the
suburbs, with large homes spread apart by manicured lawns. Her school was
depicted as a modern structure, with well-kept athletic fields and an inviting
playground. This Hannah's parents were college graduates. Her father was an
attorney; her mother a freelance writer.

How do you think the two groups of college students rated Hannah's
  ability?

The students viewing Hannah as coming from a lower socioeconomic
background judged her to have less academic ability than the Hannah seen as

coming from a higher economic background. The researchers concluded that stereotypes influenced the judgments.

> *Besides social class, what other types of stereotypes might influence first impressions?*
> *How might people become aware of the influence of stereotypes on their first impressions?*
> *How might people who are at risk of being stereotyped cope with the threat of being judged negatively?*

Research (Bacev-Giles & Resshma, 2017) on first impressions formed online showed that like in-person, people made judgments quickly with very limited information. They tended to view others positively who were similar to themselves. Stereotyping was common.

> *How would you compare first impressions made online with those made in person?*

Physical Attraction

Physical attractiveness can strongly influence first impressions, as Sumerlin and Lee's works stated earlier in this chapter.

> *What physical features do you notice first?*
> *How would you describe someone who is physically attractive? What would they look like?*

Most people in a given culture agree on the characteristics for physical beauty (Marcus & Miller, 2003).

> *How is physical attractiveness defined culturally?*
> *Where do we see these cultural definitions portrayed?*
> *Do you think "beauty is in the eye of the beholder"?*
> *How are people who fit cultural standards of beauty judged?*
> *What stereotypes are presented about them?*

Stereotypes can be negative, positive, or neutral. They constitute judgments that are made quickly at first contact. People who fit a culture's standard for attractiveness may have advantages over those who do not.

> *What advantages do people who fit attractiveness standards have over those who do not?*

What are their disadvantages?
What gender differences exist?

Some researchers (Busseri et al., 2006) suggest that being able to experience attraction is a sign of healthy adolescent development. This holds true whether a person has heterosexual, bisexual, or same-sex attractions.

How might physical attraction to someone be healthy?
How might it be unhealthy?
What is it like to talk about physical attraction with peers of the same gender? With peers of another gender?
When do discussions about physical attraction become unhealthy?

Flirting

Examining such a common behavior as flirting in a peer group with adult facilitation is an experience few youth ever had or perhaps even considered having. As a teacher, you may feel fortunate, grateful, and quite responsible for doing your part to make this helpful to them.

Start by defining *flirting*, which is not as easy as it seems. Students said that it could be verbal or involve touch, in-person or through texting, and indicated attraction to the other person. Build your discussion from these questions.

What's the purpose of flirting?
Is it fun?
Is it always fun? When isn't it fun?
How can you tell when a person is flirting with you? Are there times when it's unclear? Can you cite an example?
Are there times when a person is unaware that what they are saying or doing is being perceived as flirting? What are some examples of this?
Are some people able to flirt more openly than others? For example, can youth who are LGBTQ act as freely as those who are cisgender and heterosexual to flirt in public?
Have you noticed gender differences in flirting? What have you observed? Why do these differences exist?
How do people flirt by texting? Are there other ways of flirting online?
What kind of flirting would not be okay?
What's the best thing that could happen from flirting? The worst thing? What usually happens?

Flirting via Text

This adapted activity (Cooperman, 2014) examines how teen texting operates through the medium of text messaging. Divide the class into four groups and distribute a different scenario to each group. Instruct them to identify the names, gender, and sexual orientation of each character and to construct a dialogue of the characters texting each other.

Scenario 1

A ninth-grader has a crush on someone in one of their classes. This is the first time this person has ever sent a text message to someone they liked this way. They are unclear on the concept.

Scenario 2

A tenth grader finds a person they saw on social media to be quite attractive. They don't know each other. The tenth grader introduces themselves via text.

Scenario 3

A junior has a sexual attraction to a classmate and indicates this via text to that person.

Scenario 4

A senior thinks it might be fun to go out with a ninth grader to show them what high school can really be like. The ninth grader is flattered to receive this attention.

Ask the groups to present their dialogues to the class for review and discussion.

How did you decide to assign the characters' names, genders, and orientations? What factors did you consider?

How easy was it to write the scripts?

How realistic were they?

Earlier, we said flirting could be fun. Which of these seemed to be fun? What made them fun?

Which weren't fun? Why?

How could someone respond to a text from someone who seems to be attracted to them? What about responding to sexual attraction or come-on via text?

Which of these texted scripts do you think would likely bring the people together? What contributes to this?

Which scripts would probably not be followed up on?
How would these texted conversations differ from in-person dialogues?

* * *

Reprinted with permission from *Unequal partners: Teaching about power, consent, and healthy relationships, Fourth Edition, Volume 1.* © Copyright 2016 by The Center for Sex Education. For more information, please visit www.SexEdStore.com.

Getting Our Attention

Attraction doesn't just involve looking at physical appearance. There are other factors that influence a desire to get to know a person better and to begin the process of viewing that person as a potential relationship partner (Miller & Perlman, 2009).

Reciprocity can play a role. We tend to like people who like us, returning the favor, so to speak.

How many of you have heard in your conversations with friends, that
    somebody likes somebody else (as a potential romantic partner)?
How might someone react to hearing that someone likes them?

Reciprocity means that if someone hears that someone else likes them, they may reciprocate the liking; they might like that person back.

How many of you have observed this reciprocity happening at the start of
    a relationship?

A factor related to Lee's (1988) *Pragma* style, being practical, is attraction that comes from being in close proximity to someone. If you live in the same neighborhood, go to the same school, have the same classes, and generally are near each other a lot, there is a greater chance that you will develop attractions. It's just logical, as someone with a *Pragma* inclination might say. People tend to like those who are nearby. They may become your friends and sometimes your relationship partner.

How true is this among folks at this school, do you think?
Have you heard the saying, birds of a feather, flock together?

Connections can begin from discovering similarities between you and another person. People tend to start relationships with those who are around the same age, have similar beliefs and attitudes, share common interests, and have similar personalities (Miller & Perlman, 2009). There is even evidence that people who have similar physical attractiveness have a greater tendency to engage in romantic relationships (Jackson et al., 2022). Having things in common may help build expectations that things will work out.

How might these similarities foster the start of a relationship?

On a conscious or unconscious level, starting a relationship may involve assessing the rewards one may obtain by being with a person. This might be things you get from that person directly, like their interest in you or having fun with them. Rewards might be indirect, like being with that person gains one entry to their group of friends or their status in the school. The expectation that something good will happen to you from being in a relationship with that person may be a motivator for seeking this relationship.

What do people hope to get from a partner at the start of a relationship?

Communication at the Start of a Relationship

An important goal of communication at the start of a relationship is gathering and disclosing personal information. We recalled the Johari Window (Luft & Ingram, 1955) construct from an earlier session.

*What are the first things you want to know about a person as you prog-
ress beyond the contact stage and start to consider the potential for a
relationship?*

Early communication also aims to find common ground, which tends to occur though small talk. This superficial conversation can be more about broader topics rather than in-depth discussions.

What are examples of small talk?
*What are some opening lines a person can use to engage another in
small talk?*

A step beyond small talk is engaging in surface contact. This probing for common ground and shared interests also involves checking out feelings of attraction on both sides. Divide the students into groups to come up with skits providing samples of surface conversations. Have them act these out in the class and discuss after each skit.

Is this relationship going anywhere?
How can you tell?

Look at a factor you discussed earlier: reciprocity. Again assign them to create and act out a skit that involves demonstrating reciprocity in a surface contact.

Did you witness reciprocity?
Are there mutual exchanges where compliments are given and returned?
Did you hear positive words from one person spark positive words from the other?

Asking Somebody Out / Being Asked Out

Youth experience different levels of risk-taking when it comes to asking somebody out on a date. Being asked out spurs feelings as well, although being the initiator is arguably the more threatening since rejection is a possibility.

What are some feelings that people have when they're thinking about asking someone out?
What considerations do they have to make before they propose going out? In other words, what do they have to think about ahead of time?
What role might friends have in this?
What do you think it's like being the one asked out?
What feelings might they have?
What are the possible outcomes of asking someone out?

Students generated these possible outcomes:

The person says yes unconditionally.
The person says yes but has conditions (where to go, how late to stay out, who's coming along).
The person says no and closes the door to ever dating that person.
The person says no but leaves the door open (I'm busy that day, but maybe some other time).
The person says no and is ambiguous about ever going out (I can't go and I don't know about later).

Discuss the different reasons and feelings that might be associated with each possibility. Assign breakout groups for the students to develop and act out skits. Give each group a different outcome. Ask them to portray the scenes to include settings, characters, actual dialogue, and emotional experiences.

After the skits, discuss how realistic they were, how else might events occur in the scenes, and how the asker and the one asked could obtain support from others.

> *A friend tells you they want to ask out someone they are attracted to. They are a little nervous about it. What's your advice?*
>
> *A friend is being asked out and they're not sure they want to go. They've delayed their answer to that person in order to get advice from you. What do you say?*

Starting in Secret

Some youth begin relationships in secret. They partner with another person but neither tells anyone that they are a couple. When presented with this possibility, students affirmed the reality of such experiences. Research indicates that such secrecy had mostly detrimental effects on the individuals involved and the relationship itself (Lehmiller, 2009).

> *Why would people want to keep a relationship secret?*
> *What would keeping it secret tell you about the relationship?*
> *What effects would secrecy have on the relationship?*
> *What burdens does it place on the partners?*
> *How does keeping secrecy affect the commitment people have to the relationship?*
> *How does it affect the logistics of seeing each other?*
> *Does it pose a threat to partners' psychological health? Personal health? Self-esteem?*
> *How might secrecy benefit a relationship?*
> *When might a couple come out to others? What would make them decide to?*
> *How long can a couple keep a relationship secret?*
> *What advice would you give a friend whom you think is in a secret relationship?*

To summarize, this chapter addresses themes, issues, feelings, and skills pertaining to the start of a romantic relationship. By focusing on the processes that typically occur during this early stage, youth can examine how to strategize and evaluate their first steps.

Chapter 8

Communication Skills

By this time, students develop a high investment in the course and are motivated to delve into this important skill-building. Such training is rarely available to youth unless they participate in a counseling program or something similar. Be motivated to bring this to them.

Teaching communication skills is similar to other kinds of skill-building. It involves a didactic component (steps and techniques), modeling, and repetition through practice. The emphasis is on the skill and less on the content being used to learn the skill. So you sometimes drift away from relationship content in order to focus more explicitly on a skill. The sequence of training is adapted from a program used with university residence counselors (Jandernoa, 1973).

The *Fortune Cookies* meditation (Luck, 1992) provides an appropriate start to open students' minds to the need and importance of communication. The imagery and instructions have the listeners say something positive to themselves, something they need to say to someone else, and something difficult to communicate. It gives students access to a unique way of experiencing communication.

LISTENING SKILLS

Ask students to write their names on slips of paper and put the slips into a box. Draw their names for the activities that follow. As your group agreements state, they always have the right to pass. No one ever did.

For the first exercise, draw a name and ask the student to demonstrate ineffective listening as you ramble on about a summer vacation. Considering that you are giving students the opportunity to *NOT* listen to a teacher on purpose, there may be other students asking to volunteer as well. Instruct the class to look for specific behaviors being shown. They identified lack of eye contact, turning away, interrupting, sighing as if bored, and tapping, looking at a cell phone, adjusting clothing, and other distractions.

Today we will work on effective listening, breaking it down into different practice skills. Listening takes effort.
First let's look at how we listen. In this class we will build toward effective listening skills, step-by-step.

Draw another name and ask that student to leave the room. Tell the class that they will be directing the student to draw something on the board. The first word is *tree.* When the assigned student returns, explain the task and add that they cannot look around and cannot ask questions. They are to try to complete the drawing or announce what they thought it was at any time.

Try to guess what they're telling you to draw.

After the first student completes the task, draw another name and follow the same procedure for *house.* Repeat with another student for *two-humped camel.* Leave the room so they can decide what they will have you draw. Some might feel that is risky, but trust the students and have fun with it.

What did you notice?
What feelings did you have while drawing?
What does this exercise tell us about listening? (It helps to receive clear and explicit messages. It is difficult to listen and not have an exchange to clarify what's heard).

Listening Practices

Draw more slips to divide the students into groups of 3–4. Their task is to take turns speaking and listening. The first student says 3–4 sentences and the student to their right tries to repeat verbatim what was said. Model the task by reading or reciting William Carlos William's (1986, p. 224) poem *The Red Wheelbarrow* to them and ask who can repeat it word-for-word.

After each student has the opportunity to perform both the speaker and listener roles, discuss the exercise.

What did you notice about that activity?
What does it tell us about listening? (Listening can be difficult; it takes energy and work; we don't listen literally.)

Ask the students to list qualities that make for good listening that came from this exercise. Write their responses into a document, which you can turn into a checklist and copy for their use in the next exercise.

Here is a sample list. Add any characteristics you think are important that they omitted.

Maintains eye contact (not staring)
Gives non-verbal signals that they're listening (nods head, leans forward)
Asks questions
Rarely interrupts and only gently, like to clarify something said
Shows they are sincere and attentive and interested
Stays focused on the speaker
Remembers what's said earlier in the conversation
Does not distract
Doesn't look at their cell phone when someone is talking

See Figure 8.1 for a sample checklist converted into an observation record.

Ask the students to identify five things that would be interesting to know about a classmate and write these on the board. Some examples to give them include:

Your most difficult school assignment
Something you'd like to change about this school or agency
Something you're proud of about this school or agency

Draw slips to divide them into triads. Using their list as content, have them practice listening. One person chooses something from the list to speak about, another person acts as the good listener, and the third student observes and records feedback on the listening checklist. The speaker talks for two minutes (time it), then the observer gives feedback. Encourage them to converse about the listening experience. Then rotate roles so each has an opportunity to listen, speak, and observe. Process the exercise with the entire group.

What did the listeners do well?
What did you learn as an observer?

The next practice involves summarizing what they hear.

Summarizing means stating in your own words what you heard the speaker say. At the end of their statements, you try to capture in your own words a version of the key points the speaker made. By doing this, you let the speaker know you were listening, you provide an opportunity to be clear on what was

Listener	1 Excellent	2 Good	3 Fair	4 Poor	5 Not at all
Faced the speaker and made good eye contact.					
Gave nonverbal signs that they were listening.					
Asked questions to clarify what they heard.					
Showed that they understood the content of what the speaker said.					
Complimented the speaker.					

What suggestions would you have to improve the listener's skills?

As an observer, what did you learn (or re-learn) about listening?

Figure 8.1.   Basic Listening Observation Check List

said, and check your understanding with the speaker. Some people use the term paraphrasing instead of summarizing.

Provide some phrases that can be used to begin paraphrasing from a book on communication skills for youth (Skeen et al., 2016, p. 14).

> *"I heard you say . . . "*
> *"In other words . . . "*
> *"I understand that . . . "*
> *"Are you're saying that . . . "*

"What happened was . . . "
"Are you telling me . . . "

Repeat the same practice process, adding summarizing to the checklist. Ask the students for new things to talk about. Here are suggestions.

A decision that requires considerable thought
Something you've done for an older person
Something you did to express your individuality

The next practice involves reflecting feelings heard in the speaker's statements. Maybe the feelings are stated explicitly, or maybe there are feelings picked up from facial expressions, tone of voice, the content of the remarks, or from one's own intuition and understanding. Stating the emotions you sense being expressed is an advanced form of listening. Add reflected feelings to the checklist.

Repeat the practice with the trios, adding new suggestions for content.

A family tradition
A task that was difficult but that you completed
A time when you said something when it would have been easier to keep quiet

Active Listening

Active listening involves combining these more advanced skills. The listener speaks in a way that enhances understanding for themselves and the speaker. It allows for growth in the communication. Active listening requires energy, being fully present and attentive, and thoughtful feedback. It incorporates all of the skills just practiced. An active listener shows the speaker that they are being heard through clear and authentic non-verbal behaviors, paraphrases the content, asks clarifying questions, and identifies emotions without judgment. The message being given to the speaker is that the listener is open, aware, and empathic.

Again ask the students to provide ideas for the content to use for practices.

List five things that a classmate can talk about that involve an emotion of low to moderate intensity (e.g., pleasant, annoyed, friendly, and grouchy).

Listener	1 Excellent	2 Good	3 Fair	4 Poor	5 Not at all
Faced the speaker and made good eye contact.					
Gave nonverbal signs that they were listening.					
Asked questions to clarify what they heard.					
Showed that they understood the content of what the speaker said.					
Tried to understand how the speaker is feeling and reflected the feelings back to the speaker.					
Gave suggestions rather than advice.					
Complimented the speaker.					

What suggestions would you have to improve the listener's skills?

As an observer, what did you learn (or re-learn) about listening?

Figure 8.2.   Advanced Listening Observation Checklist

Form trios and use the Advanced Listening Observation Checklist (Figure 8.2) as a tool for feedback.

Verbal Communication

Follow a sequential approach to the verbal aspects of communication. Starting with assessing voice and intonation, proceed to using *I–statements*, a cornerstone of meaningful and empathic dialogue, to styles of communication, and then to types of messaging. The goals are to build skills that will be useful in couples communication and that will enable constructive conversations on difficult issues, strong emotions, and in vulnerable circumstances.

Voicing

Start with a self-assessment. Instruct the students to write responses in their notebooks to the following questions:

Is your voice high and nasal? Low and resonant? Somewhere in between?
Do you speak in a varying pitch? In a monotone?
Does your voice project well?
Do you speak too fast? Too slow? At a comfortable speed?
What do you like about your voice? What would you like to change?

Move on to some very basic voice training. Ask them to sit up straight and engage in some deep breathing exercises, similar to how you start the daily meditations.

Take a deep cleansing breath. Fill your lungs, hold briefly, then let all the air out. Breathe deeply and count back from seven as you complete one inhale-exhale set. Make sure you're breathing from your diaphragm.
Loosen your lips and jaw by humming and trilling.
Stretch your neck by gently rolling your head from side to side. Now go up and down.
Stick your tongue out, way out.
Relax your head and shoulders.
Say the vowels, slowly and distinctly (A E I O U)
Now let's experiment with emphasis—read this sentence, each time emphasizing a different word—"Are you listening to me now?"

Practice on varying the pitch, taking turns reading the following statements written on the board (or projected on screen).

Read these sentences, making your voice go up and down.

I got a B on my science test.

I'm going to the dance on Friday.
I'd love to go to the movies with you.
I don't want to do that.

Introduce the next practice, by stating, *"It's not what you said; it's how you said it!"*

When does that happen?
What does that mean?

Assign the students to work in trios, giving them three index cards for each of the following statements. Have them take turns selecting a card and to alter their voice according to the emotion on the card.

I got a B on my science test. (Proud, sad, angry)
I'm going to the dance on Friday. (Excited, bored, scared)
I'd love to go to the movies with you. (Happy, sarcastic, flirty)
I don't want to do that. (Alternate accentuating the I, want, that)

Solicit four new sentences from the class, posting them on the board. Ask them to go back to their trios and take turns using their voices to convey a different meaning or emotion as they read the sentences. Ask the listeners to identify the meaning or emotion based on the intonations.

I–Statements

Speaking with *I–statements* allows individuals to take responsibility for their own thoughts, feelings, and needs without blaming or accusing others. It opens the door, then, for others to take responsibility for what they do or think or say. *I-statements* allow the receiver of the communication some room to respond and don't force a person to be defensive. These statements tend to help maintain connection or achieve a reconnection.

How do I–statements differ from you–statements?

Examples of beginning a sentence with an *I–statement* include
I believe . . .
I think . . .
I feel . . .
I want . . .
I need . . .

I–statements are the least threatening way of saying something that may be difficult for the other person to hear. They avoid the use of second person *you–statements*, which may sound challenging, confrontational, and aggressive. In the next exercise, place the students into small groups and instruct them to replace the statement given with an *I–statement*. They may create any context they want to clearly portray their message.

You only think for yourself!
That's really stupid!
You don't really care what I think!
You shouldn't do that!
You're always trying to run my life!

Ask students to report on their work. One person reads the given statement, and the other student reads the *I–statement* that replaces it.

How did the emotional content change with the I–statement?

Have them repeat the contrasting statements, naming the emotions each conveyed.

Take this to the relational realm by asking them to brainstorm things that a partner might do that may be annoying. Form new groups and tell them to use this list to create *I–statements* that address the annoyance. I gave them this sentence completion statement as a model.

When you _____, I _____. I'd rather _____.
What do you think?

When finished, have them share their responses.

How can you remember to use I–statements when the situation warrants?

Styles of Communication

Communication styles can be categorized into passive, aggressive, passive-aggressive, and assertive types. All have verbal and non-verbal manifestations. Begin by demonstrating.

Stand with your shoulders slumped, head down, and speak in a low voice.

I really like teaching this course and working with you.

Tell them this is an example of passive communication.

What did you notice about it?
Do you believe what I said in the way said it?
What's your reaction to that statement and the way I said it?

Next stand ramrod straight, stare at them, point your finger at them, glare, and loudly proclaim.

I REALLY LIKE TEACHING THIS COURSE AND WORKING WITH YOU!

Identify this as an example of aggressive communication.

What did you notice about it?
Do you believe what I said the way said it?
What's your reaction to that statement and the way I said it?

Next stand sideways, smirk, lift one eyebrow and speak the sentence in as sarcastic a tone as you can manage without laughing.

I really like teaching this course and working with you.

Tell them this is exemplified passive-aggressive communication.

What did you notice about it?
Do you believe what I said the way said it?
What's your reaction to that statement and the way I said it?

Lastly, stand straight, but relaxed, smile, make eye contact with as many as you can, and speak in an even, clear voice.

I really like teaching this course and working with you.

State that this is an example of assertive communication.

What did you notice about it?
Do you believe what I said the way said it?
What's your reaction to that statement and the way I said it?

Write the four styles on the board and discuss the characteristics of each (Mayo Clinic Staff, 2011). Being passive means having trouble standing up for yourself and saying no. The person with this style tends to go along with whatever the group or a partner decides, avoids conflict, and is often taken advantage of. The passive style causes the person to become resentful but they are unlikely to disclose this. They may feel like a victim and may seek revenge.

The person with an aggressive style can be loud and bossy, reacting quickly and strongly to get their way. They tend to ignore others' feelings and opinions. They can intimidate, humiliate, and threaten others. They like to get even if they experience losing in any way. They are difficult to trust and experience mutual respect with.

Someone who uses the passive-aggressive approach is indirect when it comes to their wants and needs and statements. They use sarcasm. It can be difficult to understand what they actually mean. They say yes when they mean no. Over time, this style undercuts a relationship because the sarcasm and indirect language brings mistrust, confusion, and frustration to partners and friends.

Assertive communication is honest and direct, calm, and even confident. The assertive communicator takes responsibility for their own feelings and actions, using *I–statements* regularly. There is respect for others' emotions and experience. Relationships become stronger using this style as trust, mutual respect, and understanding grow.

The practice involves going into small groups to create responses showing the four communication styles for each of the following scenarios.

You stayed up late finishing your math homework. When you get to school, your friend Alex, who tells you they were up late playing a video game, asks to copy yours.

You're planning to ask Chris to the Spring Fling Dance. Before you can, Sam asks you to go with them.

Your partner wants to see a horror movie. You hate horror movies.

You go to a comedy movie with your partner. Someone cuts in front of you in line.

Ask students to share their responses with the class.

Chapter 9

Emotional Communication Skills

It's not helpful or respectful to attribute adolescent moods and behaviors to "raging hormones." Focus on their emotional experiences. It's not just biology, but the youth's history and the current context, the circumstances in the particular setting they are in and the people around them that generates sometimes intense feelings. As Jerome Kagan (2007) states,

> Emotions are like the weather. There is always some form of weather, but we award special status to the infrequent, distinct arrangements of humidity, temperature, and wind velocity called hurricanes, blizzards, and thunderstorms. (p. ??)

So, it is with adolescent "raging hormones," sexual desires, rejection sensitivity, relationship breakups, and crushingly disappointing grades. As Kagan says, emotions can change like the weather, but the key is to help adolescents better understand, learn from, and manage the behaviors associated with their emotional states. Helping them communicate about their emotions is more useful than blaming things on the endocrine system.

Emotional intelligence is a concept that credits an individual's ability to think about, seek to understand, and regulate behaviors related to emotional experiences (Mayer et al., 1997). The developers regarded such ability as a special kind of intelligence.

Explain the four components of emotional intelligence using slides and a brief lecture.

Identify Emotions: The ability to accurately identify and express emotions.
Understand Emotions: The ability to understand the causes of emotions,
*   how emotions progress, and how different emotions might occur together.*
Use Emotions: The ability to generate emotions and use them to help you
*   (get ready for a game, solve problems). What are ways people might do*

this? This also involves noting that emotions signal what we need to pay attention to. "If I'm feeling strongly about that, what's going on?"
Manage Emotions: The ability to manage emotions so they can enhance decisions, choose behaviors.

Identifying Emotions

Start with the first component of the emotional intelligence model. Distribute index cards on which an emotion is written. Make sure to create pairs of opposite emotions (e.g., anger–calm). Give a card and this instruction:

Find your opposite by acting out what's on your card—do not say the word.

Have the youth stand with their partner in a circle. First go around the circle with each pair saying their words with no gestures or other action. Then go around again, having them say the words and add actions or gestures.

Explain Paul Ekman's (1970) finding that emotions are universal, that you are connected to people across the world by the ability to feel. Continuing with the course theme of valuing diversity and the potential for connection beyond a limited *in-group*, show them a video of his research. https://m.youtube.com/watch?v=h19PzyqOxxo

Identifying emotions requires building a vocabulary for feelings. For your next activity, divide the students into small groups to list as many feeling words they could in each of Ekman's seven categories of universal emotions. These include fear, sadness, anger, joy, surprise, disgust, and contempt. Have them draw seven columns so that they can list similar terms the emotions or give them a seven-columned worksheet to use. Some groups may benefit from going online to find emotion words.

Start the discussion with one group reading what they listed in the first column. One group member can read the list while another writes the term on the board or types it into a slide. Ask other groups to add to the list.

What do you notice about the list? (Meanings differ, intensity levels differ, context matters)

Refer to the Feeling Thermometer and choose a few words for them to place on the thermometer. Briefly examine how they might identify their emotions.

What signs does your body give you to inform you of your feelings?
What thoughts might you have?
What role does memory have in helping us identify a feeling in the present?

Talk about how they might identify another person's emotion. State a physical expression and ask them to call out what the emotion might be.

TEXTBOX 9.1. PHYSICAL EXPRESSIONS

- A grimace
- Eyes rolling
- A smile
- Blushing
- Twirling one's hair

- Teeth gritting
- A glare
- Looking down
- Fidgeting

Focusing on facial expressions, show them a PowerPoint quiz https://greatergood.berkeley.edu/quizzes/ei_quiz where they have to guess the emotion being displayed. For each slide portraying an expression, there is an accompanying slide identifying the feeling and the facial muscles involved. The slide show depicts racial and gender diversity.

Understanding Emotions

A second aspect of *Emotional Intelligence* is the ability to understand the causes of emotions, how emotions progress, and how different emotions might occur together. Understanding involves mindful awareness of what the emotion is (identifying it), identifying what causes the feeling, what physical behaviors occur with it, and what thoughts are associated with it.

Distribute brief descriptions of emotion-laden situations to students and ask for volunteers to read them aloud. After each reading, ask the class to state what the emotion is and why the person is experiencing that emotion.

One time I experienced this emotion was when one of my friends decided to scare me on the night of Halloween. He hid in the bushes and waited for me to walk by. He knew I get scared easily so I was beyond pissed at him. (Anger)

In one of my classes we were answering questions for the teacher. She'd ask a question and then make us raise our hands quietly until she picked someone. I couldn't tell you what she asked me or what my answer was, all I know is that in the middle of me talking, someone thought it would be funny to call me a name under their breath. I'm not gonna tell you the word because that would make this story not anonymous anymore, but I was livid. I felt so _____.
(Disrespected)

When I snuck out of my house and was brought home by a cop, I felt _____. There was nothing I could do or say that would get me out of it. I was with a person who went through the same thing and the same consequences. My mom was extremely disappointed in me which also made me feel _____. I knew that there was nothing I could do to change anything so I had to face it and live with the look of disgust on my mom's face on Christmas Eve. She was joyful to everybody except I could tell she was upset. She forgave me and the feelings did not last much longer. I just had to make sure I didn't mess up for a while. Everything takes time but she knew I learned. (Helpless)

I was _____ about a time when a friend was at a party and was texting me at certain times so that someone knew she was fine. She was at a party where she knew NO ONE but her own friend. She wanted me to call two of her other friends that lived near the party if she didn't text me. Midnight came and there was no text or call. 12:30 came around, 30 minutes after she said when she'd text again. I wasn't sure if I should wait a bit longer or text her friends. Luckily she texted me, then called before 1:00 AM saying she left because it was too much. I was ____ about the no response and worrying about what could be going on. The feelings changed after she called and told me about the night and that she was fine. (Concerned, worried)

When I was in middle school I was _____. My mother was always working. My parents were divorced so my dad would always be working too. My day consisted of waking up too early after going to bed too late, going to a place I hate (school) with kids I had no connections with, then going home to a babysitter whom I didn't like. I wouldn't do my work because I wanted attention (I didn't know at the time but now I feel that is why). Not eating solid meals because of my stress/anxiety levels due to being made fun of at school and missing my parents. I was miserable. I was _____ about what was happening to me and what was going to happen. (Confused)

When I got my letter from the university that I was accepted I felt _____. This was my first choice school. I was so _____ about getting into my top school. For a lot of seniors, being _____ over getting into your top choice is huge. (Excited)

There was a huge building we were going into. My heart was pounding fast. I couldn't wait to see what was inside. When we got in the building we had to wait in a huge long line. As we got closer, I started to get anxious. I could barely speak. It was our turn to head in behind the huge walls blocking our view of the convention. As we passed the wall, my eyes grew. It was a jaw-dropping view. I was _____! Every video game company you could think of was there. I was speechless; I felt overjoyed. I couldn't wait to explore the stands and play all the new games that haven't been out yet. It was a gamers' dream come true. (Amazed)

Have the students work in groups to write other scenarios involving emotional experiences for their classmates to identify.

Engage the youth in a free-flowing discussion using a deck of index cards with discussion prompts. Place the deck on a desk in the center. Each student picks a card in turn and responds to the question or statement on the card. The person picking the card reads it and has first choice of answering, and then others can chime in.

Name one enjoyable and one uncomfortable feeling.

How long do feelings last? (The point is that they change)

Name two feelings that you can experience at the same time. (Note that you can have a primary feeling and a secondary feeling; the latter sometimes is a feeling about the primary feeling!)

What are some ways that feelings are triggered? (Thoughts, events, memories)

Give an example of how an emotion can drive a behavior. (Angry, punch a wall)

What might make it difficult for a person to identify what they are feeling in the moment they are feeling it? (Confusion, intensity, multiple feelings, unexpected)

How might an emotion from a past experience affect a person experiencing a similar emotion in the present? (Might increase the intensity of the moment, might cause confusion, might misinterpret the present, and might help understand what's going on).

What are some things people do to try to avoid experiencing a feeling? (Distract, activity, evoke a different feeling, defense mechanisms)

How does how we are trained as females and males create differences in emotional experiences? (Male training: Alexithymia, trained avoidance of experiencing emotions (except anger); Female training: stifle yourself, others' needs more important than yours, avoid expressing emotions that might be uncomfortable to others)

Put these in order from least to most intense: Happy, Content, Ecstatic.

Why do emotions vary in intensity?

What feelings are most difficult to express?

What feeling that someone else is expressing is most difficult to deal with?

Refer to the Feeling Thermometer and ask them whether they thought your use of this tool is helpful in understanding their feelings in this class.

Using Emotions

A third aspect of emotional intelligence is the ability to generate emotions and use them to help accomplish something.

What are ways people might do this? (You psych yourself up for the play's opening night or the big game).

This also involves noting that emotions signal what you need to pay attention to.

If I'm feeling strongly about something, what's going on? (Something important!)

Divide the students into small groups to discuss this scenario.

There is a person in your ____ class that you have been friendly with (and they've been friendly back). You want to explore the potential of taking this further. Discuss the following questions with your group and prepare to report your answers to the class.
What is your desired outcome?
What emotional state do you need to be in?
What can you do to bring yourself to that state?
What state do you want the other person to be in?
What can you do to influence the other person to be in that state? Think of statements, questions, and consider the environment and the typical emotional mood of the person.

After about 15–20 minutes, rejoin as a class and have each group report their responses.

Managing Emotions

The fourth pillar of emotional intelligence is the ability to manage emotions. This allows for better decisions and smarter choices in behaviors than those driven by emotion alone. Sometimes, people experience an intensity of emotions, a flood of feelings that can be overwhelming. The fear-experiencing part of the brain, the amygdala, is in control. Getting a handle on your behaviors during such times is a skill to learn. It has to do with using the front brain, the prefrontal cortex, to stifle impulses and let rational thinking take hold.

Explain that people can develop their own ways of expressing their emotions. They may adopt a particular style based on their personality, experience, and observations of how others behave. Talk about some of these styles using slides or writing on a whiteboard. Ask them to consider what style or styles seem most familiar to them.

Blaming: You blame how you feel on other people or the circumstances you find yourself in. "She made me angry" or "He caused me to do that."

Stuffing: You don't express what you're feeling. This may be your choice. You push your feelings away and may even act quite differently than how you are really feeling. For example, you may smile even though you are very angry.

Denying: You don't notice or are unaware of what you're feeling, even though others may detect your emotion. A friend tells you that you look upset and you reply, "What do you mean? I'm fine."

Intensifying: You express yourself with intensity, using loud, boisterous, and exaggerated behaviors. You scream with delight, explode with anger, and jump high with excitement.

Minimizing: You downplay your feelings. You ignore what information your emotions might reveal about what's happening to you. "Yeah, I'm sad, so what?"

Pausing: You think about what your feelings are telling you before deciding whether you will act or what action you will take.

Allow time for them to reflect on these styles and then discuss.

Which style do you tend to use most often?

How does the feeling itself affect what style gets used? For example, does sadness tend to be expressed a certain way? Anger? Happiness?

How are styles affected by the people you're with? Do you act differently among family members than among friends? Among teachers and a parent or guardian?

How does a setting, the environment you're in, affect your style?

Are there other styles you've experienced or noticed others showing that aren't listed here?

What are the advantages of pausing?

What constructive ways have you found to help you control your actions when you feel strong emotions and high energy? (Affirm their efforts to regulate emotions).

Further your examination of managing emotions by discussing this situation.

Drew met Christine in a Social Science class when they were assigned to a small group together. They seemed to hit it off and talked before and after class. He asked her out but she told him that unfortunately, she was in a relationship with Brian and they've been together for five months. They continued talking, however, and Christine enjoyed their friendship. Drew aimed for a closer connection. He began contacting Christine on social media. Brian found out from a friend, Kenny, about this guy who seemed to be hitting on his girlfriend. When he asked Christine, she told him they were just friends. Brian told her to end things with Drew. "But we're just friends," she told Brian. That night Brian checked social media and saw Drew's messages to Christine. He asked Kenny to join him the next day to get this Drew guy.

Divide the class into four groups and assign each a different person in the story to focus on. Ask them to refer to the four Emotional Intelligence components to develop responses and to prepare a report to the class on their assignment.

How is _____ probably feeling?
What accounts for her/his feeling this way?
What information are her/his feelings giving her/him?
How can he/she manage this situation?

After rejoining as a class and hearing the reports, ask

What is the worst thing that could happen from this situation?
What's the best thing?
What's most likely?
How might the different styles of expression contribute to these outcomes?

Conclude the investigation of communicating with emotional intelligence by linking it to previous course content.

People with secure attachment styles show warmer, more expressive non-verbal messages, with more laughing, smiling, gazing, and touching. They engage in more self-disclosure, keep fewer secrets from those close to them, and express their emotions more honestly.

End the communication training with a small group task that gives youth the opportunity to summarize their learning. Instruct each group to construct a poster, PowerPoint, or some other graphic representation of guidelines, tips, rules, do's and don'ts, or principles for effective communication in relationships. They can choose how to frame their ideas.

Here are some ideas they generated:

Be respectful, even (or especially) when you're mad.
Use I statements.
Agree about when and where you want to talk.
Stay calm.
No yelling, put-downs, or whining.
Be assertive, not passive or aggressive or passive-aggressive.
Be honest.
State your feelings and ask for theirs.
Try to understand and to make yourself understood; Be clear.
Give whole messages.
Don't give contaminated, mixed, or partial messages.
Ask questions.
Talk about what you want to keep confidential.
Take a break if you or the other person gets too upset.
Don't interrupt.
Care.

Chapter 10

Addressing Problems in Relationships

Youth face difficulties in relationships ranging from minor misunderstandings smoothly resolved to traumatic events that can be devastating. Many problems evoke strong emotions, especially when they strike key aspects of adolescent development.

Relationship problems can challenge a sense of identity. They can raise questions about being capable of love or worthy of being loved. When emotional investment is high, so is vulnerability. Conflicts that reflect a balance of power in the relationship can threaten a sense of well-being and safety. Relationships are so integral to adolescent development that problems raise the stakes for constructive resolution. The short span of many adolescent relationships attests to the struggles such challenges present.

So youth need help dealing with problems in relationships. They need skills to perceive, understand, negotiate, and resolve differences. They need help to develop awareness of their own and their partner's perspectives and strategies for dealing with conflict. They need help seeking help.

This chapter views problems as learning opportunities for youth and focuses on a strength-building approach. Encourage students to create most of the content. They know what problems occur in their lives. Respect for youth's abilities to work through even the most difficult issues centers this work.

IDENTIFYING PROBLEMS

Begin by collecting data that will provide the content for your study. Divide the students into small groups and ask them to record their responses to the following questions. Create a worksheet containing the questions for them to use.

115

What problems are common in adolescent relationships?
What problems do youth identifying as female tend to experience in relationships?
What problems do youth identifying as male tend to experience in relationships?
What problems do youth who are LGBTQ+ tend to experience in relationships?
What problems tend to occur at the start of a relationship?
What problems tend to occur later in relationships?
What problems occur when there is a significant age difference between the partners?
What problems occur with people outside of the relationship (e.g., friends, family)?
What problems occur related to sexual experiences?
What problems tend to involve the most emotional turmoil?
Which problems are the most difficult to address?

After completing the worksheet, gather as a class and share the lists. Tell them that you will use the problems they identified as content for the coming sessions. Remind them that you will be using the group agreements to guide how you work. Your intention is to learn how to address these problems constructively, not to focus on any individual student's issue, past or present.

After this session, study the issues they presented, organizing them for best use in the coming sessions. Ascertain how each problem could be addressed within the sessions. Students will be able to choose specific issues to address in the coming sessions. Separate out many of the sexuality-related problems, saving them for a later unit. You will want to adequately prepare the students to examine sexuality issues, seeking to establish safety and comfort in the classroom.

Readiness to Talk About Problems

Before beginning to dissect specific problems in relationships, examine what makes a person ready to give voice to their experience with a partner.

What makes a person able to start talking about problems?
What motivates someone to bring problems up?
What holds a person back?
Why do you think a person might withdraw from engaging in a conversation about difficulties?

TEXTBOX 10.1. SAMPLE LIST OF PROBLEMS IN RELATIONSHIPS DEVELOPED BY STUDENTS

- Arguments
- Loss of interest in the relationship/lack of variety
- No time for each other
- Jealousy
- Abuse
- Pressure for sex/sexual expectations
- Asking partner to change
- Addressing something that makes you mad/bad habits
- Communication
- Cannot fully experience the relationship
- Scared to tell others
- Insecurity
- Mental health issues
- Loss of independence
- Birth control/Contraception

- Strong differences in future plans
- Emotional Availability/reciprocation of feelings
- Comparing and competing
- Major disagreements like lying
- Proximity (living a distance away or living too close)
- Abandonment/trauma/Past traumas
- Past relationships
- Toxic masculinity/homophobia
- Using substances harmfully
- Sexism
- Family issues
- College and future planning

What can one partner do to facilitate (make it easier) for a reluctant partner to engage in a conversation about a relationship problem?

What can you apply from our earlier study of emotional intelligence and communication to talking about problems?

What might a person do to set up a conversation that has the best chance of success?

Problem-Solving Steps

This activity presents a model for addressing problems. Explain the model, going through each step using this situation as an example.

One day, your partner leaves their cell phone at your house by accident. It vibrates and you can't help but look at it. It's a text message that says, "Last night was fantastic! I've never felt so good!" When you look at who it's from, you see it's from their chemistry class study partner.

Identify the problem.
State what the problem is clearly and concisely.

Identify and weigh factors related to the problem.
What is affecting this situation?
How important are these factors?

Brainstorm alternatives.
List all ideas. Be creative.

Evaluate each alternative.
What is the best thing that could happen?
What is the worst thing that could happen?
What is most likely to happen?
Select the alternative that indicates the best possible outcome.

Implement and evaluate.
Decide how to go about implementing the solution.
Evaluate whether it achieved a desirable outcome. If not, repeat the process.

The intent here is to teach students how to use the model. Present the steps on a PowerPoint and give them a handout for future use.

Practice in Learning the Problem-Solving Model

To reinforce their understanding and help them become proficient in its use, practice some sample situations. Organize the students into small groups and give each a copy of the Using the Problem-Solving Model Worksheet (Figure 10.1).

Supply the groups with this list of sample situations and ask them to choose one for their practice. Ask them to choose aloud so that none of the other groups work on the same situation.

SAMPLE SITUATIONS

You are sick with the flu, staying in bed and feeling helpless and needy, but your partner doesn't seem to be very caring.

Define the Problem:
What is the best outcome that could occur?
What is the worst possible outcome?
What is the most likely outcome?
Brainstorm as many possible ways to address this problem as you can:
Select three alternatives that you think would give you the best opportunity to achieve the best outcome. For each alternative, create a list of pros (advantages) and cons (disadvantages) of using this approach.

Alternative 1:
  Pros:
 	
  Cons:

Alternative 2:
  Pros:
 	
  Cons:

Alternative 3:
  Pros:
 	
  Cons:

Select the alternative you think will work best. What were the reasons for your choice?
How would you evaluate whether this alternative worked?

Figure 10.1. Using the Problem-Solving Model Worksheet

Your partner's ex-partner's mother died. The mother was someone your partner knew and liked. The ex is really sad and is relying on your partner to be around the family during the funeral home visitation and funeral and such.

*Lately you've been becoming increasingly depressed and you don't really
understand why. You haven't talked very much to your partner about it.
Your partner texts you several times a day to tell you they love you. You are
getting these texts so frequently they are interfering with daily activities.*

*Lately you've been feeling that your partner doesn't understand you the
way they used to. It's like the two of you are no longer on the same page.*

*Your partner, an already busy person, has become interested in yet another
new activity or challenge. You realize that this may take even more time
away from your relationship.*

*After a long school break where you weren't together, your partner calls
and tells you they need to talk to you about something important and
wants you to come over. It can't be discussed on the phone.*

*You've had a hard day. Things have not gone well, your self-esteem is bat-
tered, and your partner does not appear to notice.*

As they work, mingle among the groups to observe how they are applying
the model. Be sure that they use the model. You may have to coach them on
some of the steps. Many groups need to be encouraged to list as many alternative solutions as they can. When all groups finish, ask the class what it was
like to use the model.

Developing Problem Narratives

In preparation for using the problem-solving model to address the list of
problems generated earlier, guide the students to develop stories or scenarios.
These provide contexts in which you will examine problems and seek ways to
resolve them. Split the students into groups and give them these instructions.

What problem are you presenting here?

*Identify the Couple. They should be high school age. Write 2–4 sentences
on each person, telling us their names, grade in school, interests and
activities, future goals, whether they have a job, and a little about their
personalities. Include pertinent information about people outside the
relationship (family, friends) who might impact the relationship.*

*Write a few sentences about their relationship, how it started, how long
they've been together, significant events in their relationship history,
what they did the last time they were together.*

*Identify the problem they are facing now. Include the context (how the
problem comes up in their lives). Tell us how each person views the
problem, what each person's perspective is on it.*

Depending on the situation, it took the students about 10–15 minutes to create each scenario. They wrote each scene on a separate paper, so that they could be shared with other groups. Mingle among them as they work, pointing out where there might be a need for clarification or elaboration in their stories. Emphasize that their stories should be realistic and avoid stereotyping any group of people. Remind them of the group agreements which include omitting names of students in the class or school.

Here are some sample scenarios developed by students.

Mary-Sue had an amazing boyfriend, so she thought. She brought Jason home to meet her parents. At first, he was very polite and respectful, but by the fourth visit or so, this changed. He began acting as if he owned their home. He would help himself to food without asking, interrupt conversations, be aggressive in disagreeing, claim the remote, and basically do whatever he wanted. My parents were getting frustrated at his rudeness. Mary-Sue talked to Jason. He said he would change. He didn't.

Susan got a really cool shirt. She slept over at her friend Jackie's one night and "lost" her shirt. A week later she sees Jackie wearing her shirt while flirting with Susan's boyfriend, Oliver. Susan confronted her and Jackie lies, saying she bought it, but there is a stain on it in the same place as Susan's shirt. Oliver stands there smirking.

*Sandy was dating Bob, but her best friend was Mike. Sandy and Bob were very close but jealousy was definitely one of the weaknesses in the relationship. One day Bob asked Sandy to hang out and Sandy kindly told him that she already had plans with Mike. Bob expressed to Sandy how upset he became when she hung out with other male (non-family) members. Sandy tried to explain that Mike was **just** her friend and there was nothing romantic going on between them. Bob listened, and then angrily punched the wall. Sandy became very upset herself and retreated to Mike for comfort. While Mike tried to soothe Sandy, Bob came in to apologize to Sandy. Seeing her in Mike's arms enraged him even more and he then and there broke up with Sandy. Later, Sandy began dating Mike and Bob regretted ever getting jealous. He realized he should have just trusted Sandy because now he was alone.*

Jayce is Black and is in a relationship with Hailey, who is White. She's an honor student and active in sports and clubs. He's really smart, but currently not in any extracurriculars. He quit basketball after a run-in with the coach and he gets in trouble a lot in school. The assistant principal in particular seems out to get him for any minor infraction. The other day, the assistant principal suspended Jayce, yelling at him in the hall for wearing a durag, claiming it was against the school dress code's no-hat policy. Jayce yelled that it was bullshit so he got suspended. Most of their friends and it seems that most of their teachers are cool with the relationship, but some people, Hailey's parents, the assistant principal, some of their friends are definitely not. Jayce and Hailey are feeling a lot of pressure.

Mark is really in love with Sheila. It's his first real relationship and he feels so lucky that Sheila picked him as a partner. They hang out a lot at school and party together on weekends. Sheila loves drinking and getting high and often gets blitzed. Mark looks after her. At one party, she got drunk and broke some decorative candles in their friends' house by pretending they were swords and smacking people with them. Mark stepped in to prevent the people she hit from fighting with her. He told their friend that the candles broke by accident and that he would pay for them. At school lately, Sheila's been high when they get together. He tells her he wishes she'd get better control of her using and she tells him if he doesn't like it, to find another girlfriend. Mark's spending less time with his friends since he was going with Sheila and feels that he's a lousy friend for distancing from them and now it seems he's a lousy boyfriend as well.

Grace is sixteen and has never had a boyfriend. She's never wanted one. She's never hugged, kissed, or done anything sexual with a guy and has never wanted to. She's been pretty sure that she's lesbian for a while now but has never done anything about it. Now she has a female friend, Hayley, who she likes very much but isn't sure how Hayley feels. Grace feels really shy and very reluctant to approach Hayley about this.

Discuss each situation presented, focusing on whether the proposed solutions are realistic, desirable, and achievable. Students proved adept at identifying the many nuances that might occur in their situations. They were well-versed in examining problem issues, and generally appreciated having a structure for their discussions. Youth sometimes want to use this format for additional problem situations so you may add more sessions for them to do this.

Infidelity

Students rated cheating or infidelity at the top of their lists of most difficult or most hurtful problems in virtually every course. It deserved to get special attention. Mindful of the intense emotions this topic can bring, begin with a rehash of the group agreements, a centering meditation (Boyle, 1993), and a word about how emotions provide information about one's experience.

Observing our feelings when we deal with an intense topic can help us learn more about ourselves.

Infidelity is defined differently by different groups of youth. Some research shows that males tend to narrow it to sexual intercourse or other sexual behaviors (Miller & Perlman, 2009). Females tend to include certain non-sexual behaviors.

How would you define infidelity? (Having sex, being unfaithful to a commitment of monogamy.)
What other words are used to describe infidelity?

People sometimes use the term, "cheating" to refer to infidelity. Cheating often involves doing something to get an advantage for some personal benefit.

What benefit does someone get for being unfaithful to a partner?
Is flirting cheating?
Is sexting cheating?
What activities on social media might be considered being unfaithful?
What gender differences, if any, do you think occur in how infidelity is viewed?
What differences, if any, do you think occur among youth of differing sexual orientations?
How many youth in relationships do you think engage in sexual infidelity?

Show the following research reports on slides.

35% reported having sex outside the relationship (Buzwell & Rosenthal, 1996).
45% reported their partners had sex outside the relationship (Buzwell & Rosenthal, 1996).
23% of males and 19% of females reported being unfaithful (Mark et al., 2011).
39% of females reported being cheated on, while 36% of males reported being cheated on (Perez, 2017).
66% of older adolescents had sex outside of their relationships (Feldman & Cauffman, 1999).

There is a lack of similar data on infidelity in same-sex relationships among youth.

What are your thoughts about these data?

Leaving these data visible to students, post the following results of studies on youth attitudes toward infidelity. Large majorities reported wanting a relationship where partners are faithful to each other.

92% of females and 78% of males desire faithfulness in their partners (Perez, 2017).

67% of college-age youth reported cheating or being cheated on (Perez, 2017).
70% of college-age youth disapproved of cheating (Perez, 2017).

Ask them why is there such a discrepancy between what youth say they want in a relationship (monogamy) and the very common experience of infidelity.

Why do youth rates of infidelity far exceed those of adult couples?

Go more in depth into the issue, with the following questions serving as primers to the discussion. Discussions varied in the classes, depending on the students' levels of experience and openness. It is important to maintain consistency with the group agreements as these conversations progress, as the level of emotional intensity can rise and overwhelm students' cognitive controls. Remind them that while personal experiences are an important part of the discussion, your main intent is to gain a clearer understanding of infidelity in a broader sense.

Who do you think is more likely to cheat? (Sample responses included: ludus and eros love styles; avoidant attachment style; having a high opinion of their physical attractiveness; gay males; gender non-conforming females; lower relational commitment; less sexual satisfaction; lower self-esteem; started having sex at younger age)

Who is more likely to be cheated on? (Being depressed; having a lower sex drive; failing to give their relationships priority by putting in the time and energy; low self-esteem; tending to see problems as their partner's fault)

Who doesn't cheat? (People with a high level of commitment to the relationship; in love; religious)

Why are youth unfaithful to their partners? (Sexual dissatisfaction; emotional links to another; physical attraction to another; opportunity,; anger and disappointment at partner; self-esteem boosted when another person is attracted to them; sexual excitement; to compare with partner; a way to breakup; being under the influence of alcohol or other drugs)

How do people learn about their partner's infidelity? (42% of partners never find out that their partner cheated on them; 60% of those find out from their partners telling them) (Perez, 2017)

Is it better to know or not to know? (Most said they would want to know)

Does how one finds out matter? (Very much so; youth talked about having the partner disclose compared with others like friends or rivals)

What emotions occur for the partner who is unfaithful? (Guilt, regret, pride, confusion, excitement)

How does the person whose partner is unfaithful feel? (Anger, sadness, disappointment, guilty, self-blaming, feeling inadequate, aggressive, withdrawing)

What are the possible outcomes of infidelity on the relationship? (Most instances of infidelity result in the relationship ending—over 80%) (Perez, 2017).

What would cause a couple to remain together after one partner is unfaithful? Can these relationships heal?

Is reconnection possible?

How might reconnection come about?

What would cause a couple to break up because of one partner being unfaithful? (Loss of trust, depression, feelings of personal desirability/ undesirability)

What would be a poor or hurtful way for the relationship to end?

What would be a way for the relationship to end with respect?

What might be some long-term positive effects for those cheated on?

Why do you think that happens?

(Youth report increased understanding of their relationship expectations and increased communication about expectations in their future relationships) (Perez, 2017).

A Student's Experience

In one course, a student began crying as the topic of infidelity was introduced. She disclosed that her boyfriend had "dumped" her the night before. It was unexpected and painful for her. Some of the students in the class knew this had happened and immediately spoke to console her. Others soon chimed in, many giving her caring compliments. She received many hugs from her peers.

The instructor asked how she felt about continuing in the session. She assured him that she would take care of herself and leave if she felt the need but that it might help her to better understand and deal with what happened. The students respected her privacy during the session, never referring to her experience during the discussion.

She took it all in until the end. When the instructor asked, *"Those cheated on tend to report having a higher self-esteem after the relationship ends and time passes. Why do you think that happens?"* She offered that the question gave her a perspective that she hadn't considered. She found it helpful and a relief from her torment. The resilience of youth never ceases to impress.

After the Betrayal

To investigate this issue further, have the students read an article from a news-letter developed by teens for teens (Marchetta, 2013). The article addresses how a teen couple, Jason and Laura, navigated and continued their relationship after Jason cheated on Laura with her close friend. Another teen couple, Nick and Julia, found that their relationship could not survive Julia's infidelity. Discuss these cases.

> *What did you think about Jason and Laura's situation?*
> *What did you think about Julia and Nick's situation?*
> *What was the key element affecting both of these relationships?* (Trust and whether it could be re-established)

Present the activity accompanying the article (Gelperin, 2013). Place signs numbered 1–4 in the four corners of the room. Read the following situations, including the four choices presented, and ask the students to move to the corner of the room that best represents their opinion of the situation. After they move, ask for volunteers to state their reasons for their positioning.

One of the situations is included here.

> *Lisa: "I cheated on my boyfriend because the relationship had become so predictable and I needed some excitement. He never found out and I'm not sure if I should tell him."*
> Choice 1: *Come clean and tell your boyfriend the truth.*
> Choice 2: *Tell him you're bored and try to improve the relationship.*
> Choice 3: *Do nothing; what he doesn't know can't hurt him.*
> Choice 4: *Break up—face it, it's over.*

Students became engaged with these discussions. If they ask for your opinion, state that there really is no *correct* answer, that responses are based on one's own values. Let the students have all the space in the room to identify and clarify their own values. Your opinion can get in the way of that happening.

Jealousy

Another common and difficult topic for youth that receives little formal attention is jealousy. Start the session by asking students to provide their first impressions of the term by completing an open-ended sentence stem.

TEXTBOX 10.2. JEALOUSY IS . . .

Sample responses included:

- Something you shouldn't be.
- A green-eyed monster.
- Scary.
- One partner being too possessive.
- Not trusting your partner.
- A sign of insecurity.

- Getting angry for some reason.
- Getting angry for no reason.
- Being afraid of losing your partner.

Present a formal definition for their consideration.

Jealousy is the unhappy combination of hurt, anger, and fear that occurs when people face the potential loss of a valued relationship to a real or imagined rival (Miller & Perlman, 2009, p. 311).

Is jealousy a sign of love or a sign of insecurity or both? (Some people might be jealous because of a real threat to the relationship, such as another person being a rival for their partner's affections. Some people might perceive a threat that is not really there.)

What is it about a person that might make them more likely to become jealous? (They may have a high level of commitment to the relationship, lower self-esteem, be more negative in how they view the world, have a manic love style, have an insecure attachment style, tend to be unhappy, tend to be suspicious of others, being very dependent on the relationship.)

Elaborate on the research on jealousy and attachment style. Researchers reported that anxiously attached individuals internalized their hurtful feelings (Sharpsteen & Kirkpatrick, 2007). Avoidantly attached individuals experienced self-doubt and sadness, and directed their anger toward their rival. Securely attached individuals tended to directly express anger at their partner, but still were committed to working things through and maintaining the relationship.

What feelings emerge for a person who is experiencing jealousy? (Hurt, anger, fear, rejection, worry, suspicion, guilt, depression, possessiveness, feel inadequate, threatened)

What feelings might a person whose partner is jealous have? (Anger, confusion, surprise, guilt, discomfort)

Has anyone been able to avoid ever feeling jealous?
Why is it difficult to eliminate jealous feelings?
Are jealous feelings valid? Why do we question whether feeling jealous is
    valid?

Brainstorm situations where jealousy might occur in order to contextualize the issue. Some of the situations students identified included:

Partner flirting with another person in front of you.
A friend tells you that your partner flirted with someone else.
Another person flirting with your partner in front of you.
Your partner comments about how attractive another person is.
You hear that another person is interested in your partner.
Your partner is spending a lot of time with someone they consider to be
    their best friend, but you wonder if something else is going on.
A person with very high status in the school likes your partner.
Partner walks down the hall laughing and close to their classmate.
You find out that your partner lied about being with another person.
You see that your partner's ex posted pictures of them together on social
    media.
You see that your partner posted pictures of their ex on social media.
Social media postings by others about your partner.
Your partner friends someone on social media without telling you.
Someone texts your partner when you're with them.
You express concern to your partner and they blow you off.

Divide the students into small groups and ask them to select a scenario to examine, seeking ways to resolve the problem. Instructe them to use the problem-solving model to answer the question,

How might people cope with jealousy in this situation?

Have the small groups report their ideas to the entire class for a large group discussion.

Some ideas that students identified in their discussion included talking honestly and openly about perceptions and feelings, honoring and respecting each other's feelings, doing things to boost each other's self-esteem and self-confidence, doing something meaningful together, talking about what the relationship means to them and where they see the relationship in the present and their hopes for the future. Some groups talked about establishing an understanding of expected behaviors early in the relationship.

Dating Violence/Abuse

Be sure to notify the school guidance department or agency counselling staff that you will be addressing this issue a few days beforehand, so they could have someone available should any of the youth need immediate support. Tell the students you will be addressing abuse in relationships beforehand. Give them a preview of how you will be addressing it in the session. Invite any students to talk to you prior to the session, noting that there were limits to confidentiality and mandatory reporting requirements that you must adhere to.

Remind them of the group agreements and encourage them to take care of themselves and seek support from others if they felt concerned about the topic. Have the phone number and website of crisis services prominently displayed in the room and remind students of these resources as you begin.

Begin by having the students work individually. Give them a one-page sheet with two columns, one headed characteristics of a healthy relationship and the other for characteristics of an unhealthy one. Ask them to check the three most important characteristics on the healthy side and the three most dangerous or troubling on the unhealthy side. Discuss their reasons for the selections.

Sample healthy traits included:

Trust each other
Respect each other's opinions, even when they are different
Always treat each other with respect
Shows concern for the partner's feelings

Samples from the unhealthy list included:

Grabbed, pushed, hit, or physically hurt the other
Makes the other feel crazy or plays mind games
Has ever threatened to hurt the other or commit suicide if they leave
Gets angry easily, especially when drinking

Invariably, a strong majority of the students selected abusive behaviors from the unhealthy list.

Another opening you can use is to post a large HEALTHY sign at one end of the classroom and a large UNHEALTHY sign at the opposite end. Read statements related to abuse and ask students to move to a spot at or between the signs that indicates their position on the statement.

Sample statements include:

Whenever my partner and I get into a fight, I'm always the one who has to apologize first—even if I think they're the one who's wrong.

If I want to go out without my partner, I have to call them first. It's like I need their permission.

My partner is always calling me "bee-yach" and his "ho." He's joking, I think and he seems to really love me. But I don't like it that much.

It's difficult to talk about some things, but we try.

My mother keeps warning me to stay away from my partner, that they're not good for me.

My partner is always trying to get me to try new things. Sometimes they're fine; sometimes not so much.

I'm not hanging out with my friends so much since I've been with my partner.

Describe relationship abuse as a one-time event or a consistent pattern of behavior in which one person in a relationship exerts power and control over their partner. Abuse can be physical, sexual, verbal, or emotional—or any combination of these.

What might be examples of physical abuse? (Being hit, bitten, shoved, hit with thrown objects)

What might be some examples of verbal abuse? (Name-calling, verbal harassment, private or public humiliation, threats)

What might be some examples of emotional abuse? (Stalking, giving the silent treatment, control over partner's choice of clothing, behavior, plans, friends)

Prevalence

Ask the students to predict the results of national studies on how many youth experienced abuse in their relationships. Then present statistics on relationship violence that are available online (Varia, 2006).

Between 21–32% of adolescents reported experiencing psychological or physical violence from a relationship partner.

21% had a partner who wanted to keep them from seeing friends and family.

64% had a partner who acted jealously and monitored their whereabouts.

In a study on same-sex relationships, 14.6% of males and 26% of females reported psychological violence, and 24% of males and 28% of females reported physical violence.

Youth were more likely to report abuse if they have been on five or fewer dates with the perpetrator. The longer they were in the relationship, the less likely to report.

What is your reaction to these data?
What surprised you by the statistics?
What makes it difficult for a partner to report abuse the longer they are in the relationship?

Guest Speakers

In many areas of the country, there are local domestic abuse support services, some of whom offer speakers to come to schools and agencies. They can present information on what constitutes abuse, why abuse occurs, reasons why someone stays in an abusive relationship, and ways to help someone in such a situation. They often provide students tips for helping friends, including getting help and developing an escape plan. Prepare the students beforehand by having them write questions to ask the speakers.

After the speakers leave, discuss the presentation and the youth's reactions. Ask the students to provide their own list of ways to help a friend.

TEXTBOX 10.3. TIPS FROM SPEAKERS

- Identify options and resources.
- Emphasize that the abuse is NOT your friend's fault.
- Respect your friend's decisions.
- Keep yourself safe!
- Never put your friend down for being with an abusive partner.
- Never blame your friend for the abuse.
- Never tell your friend they made a bad decision.
- Don't try to physically protect or rescue your friend.

Abusers

A person who abuses their partner should assume responsibility for their behavior. Experts advocate three components for offenders to engage in to learn from their mistakes and avoid any future abusive behaviors (Casarjian & Casarjian, 2003, pp. 127–39). Their approach involved having offenders:

Acknowledge what they did
Accept responsibility (without qualification)
Apologize to the person or people they hurt (if that person agrees to this and gives their permission).

Discuss their thoughts on these responsibilities and what else they would expect from the partner who engaged in abuse.

Conclude the examination of relational abuse with a small group activity. Separate students into groups with each addressing one of the following: how to prevent abuse in relationships, how to help those experiencing abuse, how to help those who committed abuse, and how friends, families, and members of a community might take active roles in addressing this issue. Have each group report their ideas to the large group. You could also end with giving students the opportunity to write to school and community leaders to increase their awareness and attention to relationship abuse.

Advice to Peers

This activity is modelled on advice columns that enjoyed popularity among youth (and adults) in past years. Such "Dear Abby" and Ann Landers columns have given way to newer responders, but the concept of writing anonymous letters seeking help remains consistent. Questions gathered from over 40 years of teaching comprise many of the following questions, along with those from students in these programs adding their own.

There are four ways to work with this question bank. One approach is to provide a one-page list of questions, divide the students into small groups, and let them discuss any issues that interest them. Second, post newsprint around the room, each with a selected question at the top and have the students individually mill around the room, writing their advice on the newsprint. Third, prepare index cards with questions on them, have the students sit in a circle and take turns drawing a card. The student who draws the card has the right of first response (or could pass), followed by others contributing their ideas. The fourth option is to allow students to select a question individually and write a one-page response. You can then post their letters around the room for others to review. Encourage the youth to refer to the problem-solving model.

Here is a selection of the questions.

My partner and I do the same things all the time. I'm getting bored with this relationship and don't know whether to just end it or do something to liven things up. What do you suggest?

My partner is really cute, but really quiet. How do I get to know my partner better, to open up and tell me more about who they are?

I am a senior and am in a relationship with a sophomore. She's really nice, but sometimes around my friends will say something dumb or immature. I see my friends reacting to this, rolling their eyes and stuff, but they don't get on me about it. Still, this bothers me. Any ideas?

My partner and I started having sex a few weeks ago. I keep hoping it will get better, but it doesn't. It's just not enjoyable. When it's going on, I just want it to be over. I tell my partner that it's okay, but it isn't. What's wrong?

My partner wants our relationship to be the best ever and keeps comparing us to our friends. Is this weird?

I think this guy I like may be saying anything just so I believe it. How can I tell whether what he's saying is real or fake?

How can someone love someone who doesn't love them back?

What do you do when a friend hooks up with your ex?

I don't think my partner is open enough when we try to talk. What can I do?

I think my partner and I are spending too much time together. What can I do without hurting the other person's feelings?

My partner seems to worry about everything I'm doing. This is leading to lots of arguments. Any suggestions?

*My partner is pressuring me into having sex. I don't think I'm ready. At least, I'm not sure. If I don't go ahead, my partner might cheat on me. I worry that after sex, my partner might be done with me. How do I know any of this for certain? And **Please**, don't just say, well, talk about it! Give me more specific help!!!*

My partner is too controlling, too overprotective. How can I get my partner to loosen up? Is it about trust?

I haven't told my partner I'm still a virgin. Doing anything sexual for the first time concerns me. Like my partner wants to do something that I've never done and I'm not sure I want to. How do I tell my partner that?

I'm in a relationship. Trouble is, I'm interested in another person. What should I do?

I've been in a relationship with my partner for a long time. It seems the longer we go on, the more difficult it is to get the truth from my partner. Is this just us or does this happen to others?

When do you let go? When should you break up the relationship?

When should people have sex in a relationship?

How much should you give up to your partner (time, friends, other things?)?

I don't like it when my partner makes fun of me in front of others. I don't even like it when we're alone. My partner says I'm just taking things too personally, or too seriously. What do you think is taking things too personally? What should I do?

My partner causes so much drama when I do something they don't like. Yelling and stuff. I feel like I have to be careful around some things. Is this normal in a relationship?

How important is it to do PDA (public displays of affection) with a partner? My partner says it's a way to show you care for each other. Like you should do it. I'm not so sure. What do you think?

My partner cancelled our plans together to be with his own friends. I think that doing that showed that he didn't care enough about us, or about my feelings. Am I right?

My partner didn't exactly lie to me, but didn't tell me the "whole truth" either. Is it the same thing?

Movie Application: *Love and Basketball*

Love & Basketball (Prince-Bythewood, 2000) is a go-to film for many topics in this course, but it fits best in this unit. There is so much to delve into, from the young couple's travails, their conflicts with parents, interactions with friends, the rich emotional life in the film, and ultimately, how they address and resolve their own conflict. Compile a list of student responses for the first three discussion questions.

> *What problems did Monica and Q experience in their relationship?*
> *What problems did Monica have with her mother?*
> *What problems did Quincy have with his father?*

Assign students into groups of 3–4. Have each group choose a problem from the lists and apply the steps in the problem solving model to address it. Encourage them to include a variety of alternative solutions before selecting what they think would be the best solution. Have each group present their report.

Movie Application: *Once*

This unique film (Carney, 2007) on relationships, set in Ireland, follows two unnamed protagonists, "Guy and Girl," as they share a love of music and a cautious interest in each other. It lends itself to the application of the problem-solving model, along with other themes, notably how two people may experience the potential of a more intimate relationship that does not find itself there. The lead song in the film, *Falling Slowly*, written by the film's co-stars (Hansard & Irglova, 2006), won an Academy award, and was worthy of a discussion on its own.

> *How did they meet?*
> *How did their relationship grow?*
> *How would you describe their relationship?*
> *What was his perspective on the relationship?*
> *What was hers?*
> *How intimate was the relationship?*
> *There is research* (Pollmann & Finkenauer, 2009) *that indicates that a couples' closeness with each other depends more on their mutual understanding than their actual knowledge of each other. How did you see this play out in the film?*
> *They decided not to deepen their relationship. How did they come to that decision?*
> *Can you think of how two people might begin a connection with each other, that grows closer, and then one or both decide to stop at some point? Why might people do that?*
> *What did you think about how the movie ended?*

To summarize, this chapter provides a structure and method for helping youth examine problems that occur in relationships. It utilizes students' own experience and observations to provide content for the discussions. Youth also examine how research and statistical data can be useful in helping to understand difficult problems such as infidelity and abuse. Throughout this examination, youth engage in a collaborative, cooperative effort to address the problems they identify.

Chapter 11

Sexuality in Relationships

In this relationships course, you will focus on sexual decision-making. Begin with an emphasis on the consent process. You will talk about the range of sexual behaviors that could be experienced and the importance of communication throughout. In discussing values about sexuality, you examine reasons why people choose or refuse to experience behaviors, the cultural and personal significance of first sexual intercourse, how sexual behaviors can be part of a self-discovery process, especially where orientation is involved, and how to manage potentially risky sexual scenarios. The students appreciate this unique opportunity to discuss sexuality with an adult in an honest and respectful format.

By locating the sexuality discussion well into the course, the sense of trust among students can be firmly established so that any discomfort about talking about sexuality issues in the group can be acknowledged when present and incorporated into the learning process. It is strongly suggested that anyone teaching a unit like this first engage in their own learning and self-examination process.

Take a university course in human sexuality. Avoid any abstinence-only types of trainings. Helpful training programs are very worthwhile, such as the annual conference and other trainings offered by the Center for Sex Education (https://www.sexedcenter.org/). This organization provides helpful resources, including a sex education lecture series and teaching methodology publications, some of which were adapted for this course. The American Association of Sexuality Educators, Counselors, and Therapists (www.aasect .org) holds an annual conference, sponsors a variety of training programs, and offers a credentialing process for professionals. Regional educators, like Maine Family Planning, provide helpful workshops and resources. A list of undergraduate and graduate programs in sexuality and gender can be found at https://positivesexuality.org/resources/sexuality-gender-studies-programs/.

Those looking for advanced training in developing their sexuality education expertise and skills can attend a Sexuality Attitude Reassessment

Training (SAR), which AASECT, among others sponsors. These specialized trainings, also known as Sexual Attitude Restructuring Seminars, are required training for professionals seeking certification. The SAR is designed to guide participants in the examination of attitudes, values, and emotional reactions to sexual issues and behaviors. The training involves viewing and discussing sexually explicit visuals, typically educational materials produced for this purpose. Ethical considerations apply to this training (Rhoades, 2007).

INTRODUCING THE SEXUALITY UNIT

Students come from diverse perspectives on every topic discussed in the course, but perhaps none more so than sexuality. Part of this is due to the piecemeal, fragmented nature of their sexuality education in school and at home and through popular media. They arrive with diverse experiences in sexual behaviors, consensual and non-consensual, many experiences to none, with a partner and/or masturbatory. Their common ground is a lack of opportunity for honest and open discussions in a safe environment.

You will rely on the build-up of trust from previous sessions. Ask them to assess how trusting they are in this class. Once again review the group agreements and ask if there are any in particular they should pay attention to in this unit and whether they needed to add any.

Start by giving them some questions to use as they mill about the room, interviewing each other about past learning. Time interactions so they don't exceed more than 2–3 minutes in order for the students to talk to as many classmates as possible.

At what grade did you first have sex education? What do you remember about it?

Did you learn about puberty in school? At what grade(s)? What do you recall?

What birth control methods can you name?

What do you think is the main source of information about sex for people your age?

At what grade in school did you learn about: Sexual orientation? Transgender? Orgasms? Masturbation? Sexual consent?

What is an important message you have received from your parents or guardians about sex?

What is an important message you have received from your teachers about sex?

What is an important message you have received from your friends about sex?

What advice would you give your ninth-grade self about sexuality?

After concluding the interviews, sit as a group and discuss it.

What was it like doing the interviews?
What was it like being interviewed?
How would you describe the opportunities you had to talk about sexuality prior to this course?
What do you think is the best way we can talk about sexuality in this class?
What obstacles might exist for talking about sexual issues in here?
What will help us talk?

Provide a brief overview on what topics you will be discussing and in what sequence. Invite their questions and comments and if you are willing, suggestions they have for omitting or adding to the content.

Consent

Inform the school guidance department or agency counselors prior to this session so they can be available should any student need to talk. Give the students a brief summary of the session the day before and invite any to see you or communicate with you beforehand if they have concerns. Provide students with information on local and national sexual assault support services, including hotline numbers.

Establishing a zone of psychological safety for the discussion of sexual behaviors begins with a construction of the meaning of sexual consent. Emphasizing the importance of explicit communication despite any discomfort, embarrassment, and lack of social role models is essential to the development of healthy relationships. Having prepared students with the previous focus on enhancing communication skills and problem-solving, you can enter into this topic with caution and confidence.

Using an adaptation from a lesson plan addressing sexual consent (Cacace & Abarca, 2016), begin by pairing up students with one trying to open the other's fist. After a 30 second trial, discuss the activity.

* * *

Reprinted with permission from *Unequal partners: Teaching about power, consent, and healthy relationships, Fourth Edition, Volume 1.* © Copyright 2016 by The Center for Sex Education. For more information, please visit www.SexEdStore.com

What did you try to get the fist open? (Most tried to physically open it)
How did you resist? (Most tightened their fist, some gave in)
Did anyone ask or give permission? (Rarely did this happen)
What do you think this activity was about? (Consent)

Next, begin building the group's definition.

What is your definition of sexual consent? (List their phrases.)

Show a video produced by police in the United Kingdom that uses tea as a metaphor for sex to present the concept for consent. https://www.youtube.com/watch?v=Gp6alIALDHA

After watching this video, what would you add to our list defining consent? (Have to say yes; have to ask; can change your mind; can't be intoxicated; has to be conscious throughout; can't be forced; have to feel safe; saying yes once doesn't mean it's yes another time.)

Next, read how Planned Parenthood (2022) describes consent, using the acronym FRIES in its definition.
Consent is:

Freely given. Consenting is a choice you make without pressure, manipulation, or under the influence of drugs or alcohol.
Reversible. Anyone can change their mind about what they feel like doing, anytime. Even if you've done it before, and even if you're both naked in bed.
Informed. You can only consent to something if you have the full story. For example, if someone says they'll use a condom and then they don't, there isn't full consent.
Enthusiastic. When it comes to sex, you should only do stuff you WANT to do, not things that you feel you're expected to do.
Specific. Saying yes to one thing (like going to the bedroom to make out) doesn't mean you've said yes to others (like having sex).

What can we add to our own definition list from this?

In earlier educational approaches addressing consent, the emphasis was on saying *no*, which became recognized as placing much of the responsibility for the consent process on the person receiving a sexual advance rather than the person making it. This newer approach promotes the engagement of both partners. The agreement to experience sexual activity requires affirmative consent that is clear and voluntary. Research shows that most adolescents support this concept of affirmative consent when taught about it (Javidi et al., 2020).

An intriguing part of the discussion in many groups centered around whether and under what circumstances affirmative consent needed to be verbal and when non-verbal consent could be sufficiently clear to meet the conditions for affirmative consent. Students varied in their opinions on this, with some arguing that asking and responding always needed to be verbal, while others indicated that a partner's passionate response to an overture could clearly indicate consent. The common ground tended to be the need to indicate enthusiastic consent.

After compiling your list of what constituted consent, create two other columns to identify what constitutes non-consent and what constitutes coercion. Important indicators under the non-consent heading include actions and words that are ambiguous (maybe, shrugs), silence, being intoxicated, and saying no. Under the coercion heading, the students listed physical force, manipulation, threats, or "mind-games," such as asking "don't you love me?"

Using the lists as reference, have the students analyze brief scenarios to assess whether consent was sought and given, the criteria used to make their judgments, and what might be done to change scenarios depicting non-consent or coercion into negotiation for consent. Outcomes could be giving or not giving consent. After using the examples provided, ask the students to write their own cases to review using the same format.

Mark drove Cathy to a private area near school to make out. He brought a six-pack and they drank some beer on the way. After parking, they began to make out in the car. Mark got on top of Cathy and began grinding. She kept moving side to side, not moving with him. They didn't speak.

Fazz and Jonah made eye contact at the party. Jonah nodded toward the upstairs, where the bedrooms were, and began walking toward the stairs. Fazz followed.

After discussing the scenarios and using them to add to your column lists, continue to talk about issues raised by the scenarios and their analyses. You can ask students to write a new scenario that gave their best portrayal of an ideal consent negotiation process. See the Planned Parenthood website for further materials on consent discussions, including videos modelling how such conversations can be undertaken.

Post this sentence stem (Cacace & Abarca, 2016, p. 114) and ask them to complete it individually.

Negotiating consent with a partner can contribute to a healthy relationship by . . .

Ask them to read their responses. This often brought home the point that talking about consent was not only about preventing unwanted or coercive sexual activity, but also about building trust, respect, and intimacy between partners. It elevated the mood in several classes after the discussion of tense and sometimes disturbing scenarios.

The last activity involves asking the students to develop a sexual consent policy for high school-age students. While such policies exist in many colleges and universities, there were none found that exist for high schools. So, create your own. Have students work in their small groups using the following questions as prompts. When they finish, ask them to present their policies to the entire class.

What is your definition of a sexual act?
What is your definition of consent?
How should a person obtain (get) a partner's consent to engage in a sexual act?
How should a person give consent to a partner for a sexual act?
What DOES NOT constitute consent?
What other considerations should your consent policy address?

The Touch Continuum

This activity (Thompson, 1987) rivets students' attention. It provides youth with an opportunity to talk about sexual touch in a structured format.

Introduce it by declaring that today they will talk about touch that two people can choose to experience.

We will only talk about touch that is consensual, that is, touch that each person engages in voluntarily and without coercion, as we discussed in the previous session. People usually do more than they talk about. Talking about touch is not well-modelled in American cultures. In this activity, you will see what it's like to talk about touch. Pay attention to the content and the process, what we talk about and how we talk about it. What emotions and thoughts come up during the discussion?

Move to the left-hand side of the white board and ask the students to give you some examples of what would constitute a type of touch that two people could experience, freely chosen, that would be the least vulnerable, least threatening, least intimate. When students ask what these terms mean, reflect the question back to them.

What does that word meant to you?

Encourage them to offer many examples. Ask them to clarify each suggestion so that they define the touch as clearly and as explicitly as possible. For example, if they say *a hug*, ask, *what kind of hug? What body parts would be touching?*

If students identify a partner's gender in a way that refers only to one orientation (boyfriend, girlfriend), remark on this, asking if the behavior would be placed at that position if the partner's gender was different. That will often result in students either identifying the gender or more often, referring to the gender-neutral term, *partner.*

After generating several alternatives, repeat their suggestions (a memory challenge for you) and ask if they could achieve consensus so that you can write the touch at the far left end of the white board. Usually, consensus is not possible, so you decide by majority vote. Write that touch on the board. Common examples offered included a high five, a handshake, a fist bump, and a tap on the arm. Students frequently included circumstantial factors, such as degree of pressure, having wet or dry hands, the relationship status of the people involved, and settings.

Next draw a line midway across the board and extended it to the far right end.

What is the type of touch that two people could experience, freely chosen, that would be the most vulnerable, most threatening, and most intimate?

There can be a long pause before the students make their suggestions. Again, insist that touches be defined clearly and explicitly. *Having* sex needs to be precisely defined which usually ends up being *vaginal intercourse.* Common examples offered included vaginal intercourse for the first time, vaginal intercourse where one partner was experienced and the other not, anal intercourse, and analingus. Once, a group identified a facial massage. Ask them as a group to choose which touch should be at the end, as you did at the left-hand side of the continuum.

After the end points are defined, ask for a volunteer to take your place at the board and facilitate the tasks of filling in all the touches they could that could fit in between the poles. Give them 20–30 minutes to do this. If more than one student volunteers, divide their times equally.

Students uniformly did a great job eliciting comments, often declaring that leading the group was really hard, due to the many suggestions and disagreements that emerged. They did well at holding their classmates to being clear and explicit in the touches suggested, using the phrase "*what body parts are touching?*" again and again.

Most often, students began at the left-hand side, listing the suggestions offered earlier and seeking consensus or majority approval for placements.

Some groups concentrated all their efforts at the left end (least vulnerable, threatening, least intimate). When you announce that they have five minutes left, they will scramble to the other end.

While the students interact, sit in the back and list all of the considerations they make in identifying touches and determining their placement on the continuum. Lists typically run to a page or more.

After calling time, ask the student leader(s) to be seated, thanking them for their work. Often, the class applauded their effort. Resume your position at the front and facilitate the discussion.

What caught your attention during this activity? What did you notice?

Were there differences in comfort levels at different times during the activity?

How might we apply a relationship theory to this exercise? How might Rubin, Sternberg, Lee, or Sumerlin's work fit?

What behaviors might you place in a different position if this were your own list?

At what point in the continuum would you draw a line defining where if a person does that behavior, they are no longer abstinent? (This drew a wide range of responses, illustrating the individual nature of that concept.)

What criteria were used to place a touch behavior on the continuum?

What factors seemed most important?

What would a couple be most likely to talk about beforehand? Why?

What would a couple be least likely to talk about beforehand? Why?

What other thoughts do you have about the continuum?

Report on the list of criteria you compiled as they were discussing the continuum with the student leaders. See Textbox 11.1 for a partial list of common factors.

While giving your own opinion on discussions like these is usually to be avoided, in this activity it is worthwhile to do so. State that the meaning given to the touch was most important because it went to the deepest motivation that the person might be aware of for that experience. Communicating that reason to a partner would, in itself be an act of intimacy and vulnerability. It would mark a high level of trust that could be present in the relationship, assuming that the meaning given was authentic.

This activity often reveals that students lack a language for discussing sexual behaviors, especially when talking with an adult. Slang terms are easier for them to use, although often inaccurate, vague, or disparaging, with misogyny emerging. Often students seem unaware of the connotations of the

TEXTBOX 11.1. COMMON FACTORS

Here is a partial list of common factors:

- Sex of partner
- Place
- Part of body being touched
- Degree of firmness
- Quality of relationship
- Public or private
- Prior experience with the behavior
- Physical comfort
- Eyes open or closed
- Penetration or not
- Whether discussed beforehand

- Safer sex or contraceptive use
- Positioning
- Clothed or nude
- Level of control
- Duration of touch
- Multiple body surfaces, simultaneous touches
- Order of touches
- Lights on or off
- The meaning given to the touch

terms being used. It offers you an opportunity to inform them of this and to provide accurate and gender and orientation affirming language.

Communicating about Sexual Behaviors

A common feature of quality sexuality education programs is training youth to communicate before, during, and after engaging in the behaviors (Kirby, 2000). Having established an understanding of basic communication skills in an earlier unit, you can apply and expand on those skills in this one.

Start by showing a brief video (TEDx, 2013) on the need to communicate with a partner about sexual experience. While intended for adults, the presentation offers important messages on the role of honesty and openness in sexual communication. The presenter, Orit Mordekovitch, emphasizes the need to talk to a partner about one's own educated and moral opinion on sexual decisions. Her message reinforces a major theme of this course, that each person has the right to define their own sexuality.

Follow the video by giving the students a perspective on different ways people communicate about sexuality. Based on the observations of therapists (Ehrenberg & Ehrenberg, 1988), patterns of communication about sexuality are established in households among family members.

Some families have a *Sex Repressive* style where communication patterns regard sexuality as inherently dirty and sinful unless sexual behaviors occur for reproduction. There is a denial of common aspects of sexual development, such as masturbation. Silence on sexual topics is the norm. Punishment may be administered to children and youth who violate these rigid standards.

Some families can be considered *Sex Obsessive*, viewing sex as an appetite that needs to be cultivated. There is a lack of boundaries, as adults may explicitly discuss their own sexual behaviors with their children and youth. Frequent allusions to sex occur, as do sexual innuendoes in daily life. This pattern may propel youth into early sexual activity.

Other families are *Sex Avoidant*. Adults in the household intellectually accept the importance of talking about sexuality, but they are emotionally unable to go along with this. They can be paralyzed by embarrassment. They may joke to hide their embarrassment or have a tendency to distract the conversation when sexuality issues come up. They may present facts to the children and youth (*The Talk*), but lack depth, meaning, emotional connection, and the erotic aspects of sexuality.

Finally, there are *Sex Expressive* families that view sexuality as a life enhancing aspect of being human. Adults acknowledge feelings, initiate discussions that include limits, responsibilities, pleasure, intimacy, empathy, and connection. There are many conversations about sexuality as with other topics in the household. Respect for the developing sexuality of children and youth is an essential feature. The sex expressive style is consistent with Sternberg's Consummate Love and Sumerlin's Integration concept.

Which type of communication have you observed most frequently?
Which type seems to occur in your peer groups?
Which type seems to occur in most movies or television shows? What examples can you think of?

To practice using the sex expressive style, set the students up in trios. Provide each triad with a list of questions from other youth. These are actual questions collected from the various sexuality education programs conducted throughout years of sexuality education work by the author.
Questions from High School Students

Is there ever really a safe time of the month to have sex but not get pregnant?
How is an abortion done?
What are vibrators and how do they work?
What is it like to have sexual intercourse the first time?

What are the beneficial aspects, if any, of jacking off?
What do people do together sexually?
What kind of sexual fantasies are normal?
What makes it difficult for girls to be clear about whether they want to have sex or not?
How can you tell if you're bisexual?
Does sex affect the mind?

Assign the roles of questioner, responder, and observer to the individuals in each triad. One student is the questioner and may choose any question from any age group. They should tell their partners which age group they are using. In the role play, they should try to put themselves in the shoes of the person they imagine asking the question.

Give a printed copy of the responders' instructions to all, which you can refer to as tips.

Listen carefully
Clarify to make sure you understand what's being asked (and to buy yourself time, if you need to), rephrase the question "Are you asking me . . . ?"
Answer clearly and simply in language the person can understand
Avoid asking about the motivation for the question until rapport and comfort is established
Check to see if the answer you gave met the person's need

Ask the observers to give feedback on how the responder used the tips and to think about other ideas for responding to the questions.

After the first practice round, gather as a class to discuss the experience.

How did it go?
What made responding challenging? What helped make it happen?
What happened to maintain connection?
What lessons did you learn from the practice about communication?

Have the students return to their triads and rotate roles until each has had an opportunity to be a questioner, responder, and observer. Regroup as a class after the practices.

What new insights happened for you from the second practices?
How would you evaluate your ability to use a sex expressive style?

During the activity, circulate among the triads, interjecting suggestions, responding to sex information needs students have regarding the questions, and offering encouragement. A challenge for students is to remain nonjudgmental when asked about some issues, such as abortion and gender restrictions. Encourage them to try to focus on the perspective of the imagined questioner as best they can.

Communication with a Partner

Revisit the issues for discussion that arose from the previous Touch Continuum activity as the content for the practice on communication with a partner about sexual activity. Show the list you compiled from their discussion (see Textbox 11.1). They can refer to the list in constructing dialogues for this practice. Ask the students to identify specific topics of conversation that the list brings to mind and list these for later use in their practices.

Present a format for communication in intimate relationships as the structure for the practice. The elements include the following.

Develop a clear goal.

What goal might a partner have for a conversation? (e.g., to use a condom; to try a new activity; to refrain from a certain activity)

Decide what communication strategies would work best.

What do you recall from our practices on communication? (Remember to use "I" statements. Think about what verbal and non-verbal messages do you want to give. Use assertive communication. Think of a way to start the conversation.)
  What might be important to pay attention to?
  What concerns do you have? What concerns do you think your partner might have?

Plan the context.

Where might be a good place to have the conversation? When is a good time?

Develop a script.

How might you want to word some of your statements or questions?

Ask for feedback.

How would you obtain feedback from your partner about the content of the conversation (your goal) and how did they think the conversation went? After discussing the format, have the students work in trios to choose a topic to discuss and to practice using the format to develop a script. Mingle among the groups as they work. When they feel comfortable with their conversations, gather as a large group and have them present their dialogues to the class. Discuss each scenario.

What would be the likely outcomes of this conversation?
What other ways might this topic be approached?
What might occur that is unexpected? How might this work out?
How the might this conversation affect the relationship?
How might the partners demonstrate respect and empathy during this conversation?

Examples of Student-Identified Topics for Conversation

Deciding whether to engage in a particular sexual behavior
Dissatisfaction with a sexual activity ("I don't like it when we do x" or "I'd prefer if we didn't do y")
One partner has more frequent sexual desires than the other
Partner uncertain about doing something
Telling a partner that they are a bad kisser
Saying no to a behavior one person doesn't want to do
One partner wants the other to take more initiative in their sexual activities
A partner wants the other to slow down
Concern about partner's use of porn
Use of protection (contraception and/or safer sex)
Female partner thinks she may be pregnant
A partner was unfaithful
Maintaining privacy (what's okay and what's not okay to tell others)
How using substances (alcohol, weed) affect sex
Wanting to change the routine of when, where, how they have sex
Couple had been having sex, but one partner wants to hold off on sexual activity for awhile
Partner not feeling satisfied, not having orgasms (or too few orgasms)
Partner wants more affectionate, less "lusty" sex
A partner wants to convey that all touching does not have to lead to sex
A partner wants to talk about past sexual partners; the other does not
What "being in the mood" means for each partner

What sexual activity means to each person

The First Time

While the average age of first sexual intercourse has increased in recent years, it remains an important topic of conversation among youth. According to the Centers for Disease Control (2020), 38% of adolescents experienced their first vaginal intercourse in 2019, compared to 46% ten years earlier. These data do not reflect differences among adolescents based on gender, sex, race, ethnicity, religion, socioeconomic status, area of residence, pubertal development, attachment style, and other intersectional factors. For example, African American youth report first intercourse at earlier ages than other groups (Biello et al., 2013), while Asian American youth report initiation of sexual intercourse at later ages than other groups (Hahm et al., 2006).

There are powerful cultural messages about "doing it" for the first time, which usually refers to vaginal intercourse. For girls, it's often about losing or giving up their virginity, as portrayed in films like *American Virgin* (Kilner, 2009). For boys, it's a sign of masculinity or lack thereof. The humor in the movie about a 40-year-old virgin (Apatow, 2005) highlights this gendered expectation. Full analysis of cultural messages about virginity and differences due to intersectionality requires a more in depth examination that was beyond the scope of this course.

Focus your discussion on consensual first-time sex. To examine messages about "the first time," present an activity that has students moving on a continuum to express their points-of-view. Draw a line on the board running from one end to the other. Have them move to a spot on the continuum as you define the parameters, that is, the end points on the line. Ask why they chose their point on the continuum. In this way, students can see as well as hear where their classmates stand on each of the issues. The center area demonstrates uncertainty or mixed views. Students move around the lines for each pair of opposites.

At this end, people plan having sex for the first time; at the other end, people find that their first sexual experience "just happened."

At this end, people are clear and confident about having sex for the first time; at the other end, people are uncertain or ambivalent about having sex for the first time.

At this end, people expect to experience pleasure having sex for the first time; at the other end, people expect to experience pain having sex for the first time.

At this end, people expect having sex for the first time to be an incredible experience; at the other end, people expect having sex for the first time to be something to get through.

At this end, people feel proud after having sex for the first time; at the other end, people feel guilty after having sex for the first time.

At this end, people are sober when having sex for the first time; at the other end, people drink alcohol or use other drugs before having sex for the first time.

At this end, people have sex for the first time with someone they love or care about; at the other end, people have sex for the first time with a casual acquaintance or someone they just met.

Different gender expectations emerge in this activity. Female youth tend to anticipate primarily negative emotions for first intercourse, while idealizing their love for their partners. For their part, male youth felt more eager and positive about the upcoming event and were less inclined to see first intercourse as a romantic experience or expression of true love. Male youth reported more experience and comfort with the sexual functioning of their bodies by having masturbated earlier and more often than their female partners (Martin, 1996). Approaching the decision to have sex, female youth faced the no-win dilemma of being labelled a *prude* or a *slut* (Tolman, 2002), while male youth faced performance pressures, but anticipated male peer approval (Castleman, 1989).

Female youth face the dilemma of negotiating between the reality of their own sexual desires with the struggle to maintain a good reputation and positive self-image. They face pressure to make pleasing a male partner the priority, while seeking to protect themselves from unwanted pregnancy, sexual assault, and infections (Vance, 1984). Male youth are indoctrinated into a fantasy model of sex that objectifies their own bodies and their female partners' and proscribes a domineering and self-centered sexual persona and an entitlement to sex from a partner (Zilbergeld, 1999).

How did these themes appear in our continuum conversations?
How do these themes affect people's own real experiences?

To overcome these detrimental societal messages, reiterate a primary theme and objective in the program:

People have a right to define their own sexuality.

An essential corollary to this theme is the need for an inclusive view of what behavior or behaviors constitutes "the first time" beyond a binary, cisgender, heterosexual model. Even for those youth with these intersectionalities, the need to determine one's own sexuality should be free of gendered restrictions and proscriptions.

Return to the Touch Continuum to help sort this out. Re-post their continuum for review.

Have them look at the most intimate (right) side of the continuum. Ask them to think about what behavior would be a significant *first time*. It may be vaginal intercourse or it may be something else. The option to not identify *any* behavior is valid.

> *What would make that behavior special?*
> *What reasons would a person have for experiencing that behavior?*
> *What meaning would that behavior have?*
> *What would be the best outcome for experiencing that behavior for the first time? The worst outcome?*
> *What would make it enjoyable?*
> *What might make it disappointing?*
> *What might people do to experience a good outcome?*
> *How might this first experience affect the relationship going forward?*

Movie Application: *Coming Soon*

As a relatively rare look at sexual discovery from a female perspective, this film (Burson, 1999) tells how four high school seniors negotiate gendered and heteronormative sexual scripts before liberating themselves to define their own sexuality on their own terms. Three female friends and a male classmate support each other's paths to find what is important and the meaning of sexuality in their romantic relationships.

> *Describe Stream's exploration of her sexuality. How did others' define her sexuality? How was she able to accomplish this for herself?*
> *For Stream, having her first intercourse seemed like it was about "joining the club" or "getting it over with." What influences feed those reasons?*
> *What sources of information about sex did Stream access? What is your assessment of those sources?*
> *The scene where Stream has oral sex with Chad is immediately followed by a scene of Jennifer having sex on top of her male partner (played by Ashton Kutcher). What's similar about those scenes?*
> *Why does Stream have oral sex with Chad?*

Thinking about the party at Chad's house, how did substance use affect the sexual experiences? How else might substances affect sexual activity?

When Stream confronts Chad, she accuses him of being manipulative. What does she mean?

What affected Jennifer's sexual development? Do you think she was able to define herself as a sexual person? Why or why not?

Describe Nell's sexual journey. What does she deal with in her coming out process? Do you think she was able to define herself as a sexual person? Why or why not?

Some characters lie about their sexual experiences. Why are lies told about having intercourse when they didn't? Why lie about having an orgasm when it didn't happen?

Who's responsible for a person's orgasm?

What did Stream's mother do that was not helpful to her? What was helpful?

Sexual exploration is about saying yes and saying no to activities. Who said no? Why? (When Stream and Henry rolled in the mud, Stream asks Henry to kiss. He says that wasn't what he was thinking. What do you think he was thinking about?

Henry accuses Stream of being overly influenced by her friends. How much influence do females have on each other's sexual exploration?

Jenn suggests that Stream go out with a 40-something man. Many female youth go out with older males. What do you think that's about?

What is the difference between doing sex to someone, doing sex for someone, and having sex with someone? Provide examples from the movie for each.

What were the messages about masturbation in the film? What messages have you heard in real life?

What other issues or topics raised in this movie might be helpful to talk about?

Movie Application: *The Cake Eaters*

A student strongly recommended it to complement the discussion on *the first time*. The film (Masterson, 2007) avoids the stereotypes of the adolescent male-centered story line, demonstrating instead a male youth's uncertainty about being ready for sex and a female youth's assertiveness in being ready.

Two adolescents, Beagle and Georgia, share a path that leads to their having first intercourse with each other amid the cacophony of their families' unravelling interconnections. The complications following Beagle's mother's death and Georgia's terminal illness present emotionally intense challenges.

What did Beagle see in Georgia? What attracted him to her?
What did Georgia see in Beagle? What attracted her to him?
Did Georgia want anything from Beagle besides sex? If so, what was that?
What did Beagle want from Georgia?
After getting to the motel room, Beagle initially declines to have sex with Georgia and she demands that he leave. Why did he say no?
Why did she throw him out?
Why did he come back? Why did she welcome him back?
How did having sexual intercourse affect their relationship?
What do you think of the timing of their decision to have sexual intercourse?
How would you describe Beagle's relationship with his older brother?
Beagle was upset upon discovering that his father had had a long affair with Georgia's grandmother, beginning when Beagle's mother was alive. What does this tell you about Beagle?
What does it say about the father and the grandmother?

Television Application: *Beverly Hills 90210*

The second episode of Season Two (Attias, 1992) presents several sexuality issues for discussion. The school board debates whether to allow condom distribution, with a split among parents in opposition contrasted with the pro-condom stance of students. Sexually transmitted disease, unplanned pregnancy, abstinence from sexual intercourse, a pregnancy scare, and valuing privacy are some of the many topics that are dramatized. In schools and agencies where condoms are available, students may have had experience with this issue first-hand.

Why is there such controversy about condom availability? What viewpoints have you heard?
What assumptions are made about a youth who supports condom availability?
What assumptions are made about a youth who opposes condom availability?
Brenda wants to write a paper about her pregnancy scare. Why is that important to her?
Dylan does not want Brenda to write the paper. What are his reasons?
What messages does the show give about being a virgin?
What beliefs and values do the characters have about sexual experiences at their age?

Concluding Activity: The Sexually Healthy Relationship

Having examined sexuality in relationships through a variety of thoughtful communication activities, use a different methodology to wrap things up. Provide students with poster boards and a variety of art materials. Give them a choice to work individually, in pairs, or small groups to illustrate through art their conception of sexual health. Ask them to first sit and reflect on what they had experienced and talked about in the unit and to gather their thoughts.

Each class created an array of impressive illustrations. Common themes included consent, inclusion of LGBTQ+ perspectives, intimacy, caring, openness, and respect. Post their work in a public area where other students can view it. Students in the course were quite proud of their work.

Chapter 12

Endings

The final unit of the course addresses endings in relationships and concludes with the ending of the course and the relationship you have built as a class.

In a given academic year, adolescent romantic relationships in a high school can appear to be too numerous to count. Researchers also have difficulty getting a handle on the number of adolescent romantic relationships. In national samples, one study found that 68% of youth had been in a romantic relationship by 11th grade (Furman & Hand, 2006), while another reported 59% at that grade (Giordano et al., 2006). These researchers found that relationships lasted an average of four to over 20 months, respectively.

Youth in these groups reported similar numbers. Some felt that three months was closer to the average length. Students also reported that most had been in 4–5 relationships from ninth to twelfth grade.

The point here is that start-ups and break-ups, if not daily occurrences, are certainly a ubiquitous part of the fabric of school life. You talked about how romantic relationships begin in chapter 8. Here you will talk about how they end. You will examine approaches to ending processes that promote mutual respect and closures that allow partners to leave with dignity intact.

WHY RELATIONSHIPS END

Begin your work on this topic by identifying reasons why relationships end using a simple brainstorming exercise. Ask them for reasons and as they state them, write their responses on the whiteboard. Here is a sample selection from youth groups:

Emotional Responses to Breaking Up

Ask them to identify feelings that youth might be experienced based on these reasons. In some groups, they quickly noted that the emotional experience

TEXTBOX 12.1. WHY RELATIONSHIPS END

Here is a sample of reasons from youth groups:

- A partner found someone else
- Abuse/violence
- Emotional abuse
- A partner moved away
- Going off to different colleges
- One partner realizes the other isn't a good choice
- One partner goes off to college, the other stays home
- Boredom
- Too many arguments
- Friends don't like the partner
- Parents don't like the partner
- It just happens
- One partner more invested in the relationship than the other
- Unmet expectations
- One seems to value friends more than being with the other partner
- Differences in sexual desires
- Different Love Styles (Lee)
- Different life goals

depended on several related factors, including whether a person was the one initiating the break-up of the one being broken up with, the level of commitment to the relationship, whether sexual activity had occurred, whether the break-up was sudden or seemed predictable over time, how well adjusted a person was in general, friends and family support, classmates' reactions, and the dynamics of the break-up (how they found out, what was said or done).

Refer to these those variables and ask them to list other emotions that might be experienced. Explain that they will be creating scenarios that combine various factors so that they can investigate the complexity of break-ups.

As the students offer their ideas, gently prod them to elaborate and go into greater depth.

What would cause a person to feel that?
What information is that emotion giving the person?
What do you notice about this list?
How might a person experience more than one emotion? Can you give an example?
Which emotions would be most difficult to deal with?
Which emotions would show that a person was recovering or on the road to recovering from the break-up?

TEXTBOX 12.2. EMOTIONS AFTER BREAKING UP

Feelings they identified at this point included:

- Sadness
- Relief
- Depression
- Devastation
- Anger
- Bittersweet
- Despair
- Guilt

- Shame
- Distress
- Rage
- Insecure
- Surprised
- Grief
- Contentment

- Confusion
- Feeling inadequate
- Feeling rejected
- Jealousy
- Lonely
- Miserable

Communicating about Breaking Up

To examine how break ups actually occur, you will be focusing on the dynamics of communication. Point out that ending a relationship is a process, not just an event.

How do you know when a relationship is over?
What signs might appear? (Increased arguments, disagreements; change in how often communication happens; change in tone how they talk to each other; spending less time together; any abuse)
What are some ways that an end is communicated?
What emotions would a person likely have if the break-up went poorly?

Revisit the list of reasons why relationships end, putting aside that of violence/abuse for later consideration. Ask students to select a reason and create a scenario that shows a breakup with an unsatisfactory (bad) ending. Collect their written work to distribute later to different groups.

What emotions would a person likely have if the break-up went as well as possible?

Ask them to recall their examination of emotional intelligence. Emotional intelligence helps a person to observe what they are feeling, understand it and manage emotions so that what is said and done is the result of thoughtful deliberation.

Remind them of the communication skills practices, using "I" statements, conveying complete messages, assertiveness, and active listening.

How can we apply what we've worked on to the breaking up process?

Present the following guidelines for their consideration and to use in role plays.

Suggestions for Breaking Up

These guidelines apply to situations other than when violence or other abuse is occurring.

If possible, make the first move once you realize the relationship isn't working and can't be saved. Staying in a doomed relationship just prolongs dissatisfaction and misery and avoids the inevitable.

Communicate face-to-face.

You both deserve to end this with fairness, courtesy, and consideration, honoring the value that the relationship once held for both of you. Texting, phone calls, email, or having others communicate the ending does not provide for a clean closure.

Be the one that communicates to your partner that the relationship is over.

Having someone else tell them contributes to hard feelings and doesn't allow for a clear and sensitive closure. A person may talk things over with family members or friends prior to breaking up but make it clear to your support system that you want the partner to hear about the break up from you first.

If you are the person being told the relationship is over, listen respectfully. Respond with "I" statements.

Be aware of what the person is saying and pay attention to your feelings. Realize, as quickly as you can, that the relationship is over. You will need time afterward to process the conversation and what the ending of the relationship means to you. Try as you can to be in the moment as the relationship ends.

Be honest about the reasons for ending the relationship.

Use "I" statements which are the best way of presenting difficult information. Try to avoid blame. "I felt *this* when *that* happened."

Avoid giving in to second chances.

This conversation is about ending. Promising to keep trying when you've already decided this should end is self-defeating. Reconciling with a partner is a very different conversation than this one.

Disconnect and Disengage.

This is an ending. It is about moving apart. Don't delay or end things slowly. It's over. You are creating space from this person emotionally and physically. Doing something "one more time," especially sexual activity, is a very bad idea.

Feel it.

Be open to what you feel as you go through this process. Your emotions provide you with information about your experience of what is happening. You are learning from this.

Take your time re-defining your connection to your ex-partner.

You may decide to continue as friends. You don't have to decide that at the time of the break up. You can give yourself and your ex some time to process and grieve the break up. Partners can be at very different places at the time of the break up. You also may decide later that a friendship is not desirable.

Debrief.

Carefully select people to talk to about the break up. People who are good listeners and will attend to your thoughts and feelings without judgement can be most helpful.

Distribute their earlier stories so that each group has a scenario written by another group. Have the groups take the situation with the bad ending and transform it to a situation with a satisfactory ending (good) ending. They then role play it for the class. Instruct them to apply the guidelines, their emotional intelligence and communication skills to this task.

As they work, circulate among the small groups to check on their progress and give suggestions as needed.

After each group presents, discuss the role play.

How realistic does this sound to you? What would you change to make it sound real?
How did the breaking up guidelines work in this scenario?
What do you think would go well?

What problems do you see?
What suggestions would you have for this scenario?

Here are some of the stories that students worked with.

Melissa and Brad

Melissa and Brad are together and Melissa starts to realize that she is more into girls then guys. She doesn't know how or what to tell Brad or how he will react. She also thinks Brad has been cheating on her and she doesn't know what to do about that either. Even though they have been together for almost a year, she still doesn't know how to approach this. She ghosts him.

Revised ending

Melissa decides to invite Brad over to her house when her mother is at home. She tells Brad, "I'm not really into guys anymore. I like females. I'm really sorry it turned out this way. I still care about you but this relationship isn't going to work anymore."

Sally and Austin

Sally and Austin were together for seven months. Austin flirted with other girls, which Sally didn't know about since they went to different schools. They only saw each other on the weekends at work, where they first met. Sally was close to one of Austin's friends who lived in his neighborhood.
The relationship was having problems. Austin wouldn't call when he said he would and sometimes they didn't talk for days. Their relationship was mostly based on seeing each other at work. When Austin wasn't talking to Sally, she turned to his friend. This guy told her that Austin was hanging out with other girls. Sometimes when they were on the phone, Austin would get calls from other girls and he would take them.
One weekend Sally confronted Austin about the girls and he denied everything that his friend told her. Sally talked to this friend a lot and realized how many lies Austin told her. She felt that the relationship was all a lie. Austin ended up texting her that he wanted to take a break from the relationship. She realized he didn't care for her like she thought he did.

Revised endings

When the communication started breaking down and she first heard of the other girls, Sally should have initiated the breakup then. She tells him how she feels and ends the relationship there.

She could ask for them to take a break together at work.
Sally: "I don't think this is working. I don't think we have enough time for each other."
Austin: "We work together every weekend. What more do you want?"
Sally: "I think we should do more than that. I need intimate time with you as well."
Austin: "Well, I'm busy with school and we're never in the same place."
Sally: "Exactly. It's not working. I'm sorry I can't give more to our relationship. This is over. I'm sorry. I really like you as a co-worker and friend but I can't be in this relationship anymore."

Oscar and Mace

They had been seeing each other for about ten months. They met in math class. Mace played several sports while Oscar was into video games. One day, Oscar told Mace that he decided he had enough of him and that the relationship was over. Mace was shocked and wondered what he had done to provoke this. He tried to ask Oscar what went wrong, but Oscar just ignored him. In classes, in the hallway, Oscar continued to ignore Mace.

Revised ending

Mace decided to send Oscar a text to let him know how he felt about the break-up. He wrote that he was sad and confused about the break-up, especially since it came out of the blue. He wrote that he forgave Oscar and would get on with his life without him.
At the end of the role plays, give this advice to the students.
I strongly encourage anyone who is involved in a break up, to avoid getting into a new relationship right away. Give yourself time to experience the feelings that come up about the ending and time to grieve and heal. Talk to those you trust about how you feel after the breakup. Give yourself a few months to reflect on and process what happened in this relationship. Consider what you liked about it, what you didn't, and why it didn't work out. Identify what you would do differently in the future. Clarify what expectations you have for a partner. It's important to review them again after a relationship ends.

Terminating an Abusive Relationship

Prior to the session, notify the guidance department or agency counselors so that help can be available in a timely manner for any student in need. Inform the students prior to the class, giving them an overview of what you will be covering and suggesting that anyone who thinks the session might be distressful to seek support from a counselor or talk to you privately about limiting their participation or sitting out the session if they felt they needed to. Refer to the group agreements and to the limits to confidentiality such as the requirement that you must report incidents of violence or harm to students.

Be aware that there could be survivors or perpetrators in any given class. Reflect on your own thoughts and feelings before the session so that you can focus on your role as a teacher and not find yourself responding to your own needs during the session. Reviewing tips for facilitating such sessions (Moles, 2001) can help you prepare.

The goals in this session are to provide ideas for how youth might end an abusive relationship or provide help for a friend engaged in that process. While emphasizing the importance of adult assistance, including the possibility of police involvement, remain mindful of the reality, also known to many students, that adult intervention may not prevent violent reactions to separation, as news accounts have reported.

When survivors obtain a protection order, for example, researchers (Benitez et al., 2010) found violations, which can be any kind of contact, verbal contact, stalking, or violence range from 7–81%, with greater violations occurring in rural areas and fewer violations among first time offenders. The parameters and enforcement procedures for protection orders vary among states and municipalities. The Carsey Institute at the University of New Hampshire found that protection orders can be effective in preventing or reducing further abuse (Logan & Walker, 2011). Data on violation of protective orders involving adolescents awaits research.

A concern to reflect upon throughout planning, implementing, and assessing this session involves the level of responsibility being placed on youth to address this widespread social problem. When the power of adults and institutions to protect survivors of intimate partner violence is sometimes inadequate, how can youth, with much less power, be expected to deal with it?

Nevertheless it is important to forge on, believing that ultimately talking about this issue and offering some guidance with potentially beneficial effects is worth the effort. Talk to staff from local domestic violence agencies and other resource professionals to help you prepare. Trust that the work you did in the course prior to this unit gave students a foundation of safety in the group and skills to help them move forward on this difficult topic.

Review your earlier discussion in the problems unit about what characterized a healthy and unhealthy relationship, revisiting what constitutes abuse and violence. Talk about how sometimes people in abusive relationships find it difficult to leave and may be blamed by others for not doing so.

Why might blaming the victim be harmful, or at the least, unhelpful?

Ask them to brainstorm a list of reasons why someone in an abusive relationship might stay. Compile a second list on why they might go.

What might tip the decision to leave the relationship?
When is a person ready to leave this type of relationship?
How might the decision process for LGBTQ youth differ from that of cisgender, heterosexual youth?

Ending a relationship with an abusive partner may be a dangerous time for a survivor, as the perpetrator may respond violently (Moles, 2001). Attention to one's own safety is paramount. Working with an adult, like a counselor or therapist, can aid a youth in developing a safety plan to terminate the relationship. A safety plan identifies strategies and actions a youth could take when planning to end the relationship. Walk them through such a plan (Gordon, 2021). You may want to invite a representative from the local domestic violence prevention and support services to present this information.

Contact a domestic violence support agency to help guide and support you through this process.
Identify what adults you can tell, including what adults at school that could help to keep you safe (counselors, administrators, and teachers).
Write down incidents where you were abused or threatened or felt you were in danger.
Identify safe places to go to if feeling in danger (home, school, neighborhood, work).
Arrange for a friend or adult to be with you going to and coming from school or work.
Consider changing your routes to school and work.
Have a ready excuse to use to leave if with a partner and feeling in danger.
Pre-program 911 into your phone.
Have a code word to use to communicate your danger to an adult contact.
Change any passwords that the partner might have had access to.
Change your locker at school.
Consider changing your course and work schedules.
Talk with your agency support person about informing the police.
Talk with your agency support person and the police about obtaining a restraint or protection order.
Talk with the support person about breaking up with the partner. In this context, breaking up via text message, phone, or in a public place rather than alone and face-to-face is indicated.
Keep family, friends, and trusted adults informed of what is happening.

Post on the wall of your room information about the National Dating Abuse Helpline (24/7 anonymous and confidential) Phone: 1-866-331-9474. Ask the students to copy the information into their phones.

Students tended to be very receptive to this information many commented "in case this happens." The mood in the room could be described as a somber thoughtfulness. In a few classes, some male youth became defensive when perceiving the guest speakers to be blaming all males for the perpetration of violence against girls and women. Asserting that not all males and certainly not themselves, would abuse a female partner, they sometimes lost focus on the dating abuse dynamics that were being examined.

When Parents Divorce

Many students are affected by their parents' separation and divorce. Many live in blended families. Many live in shared custody arrangements, living part of the week with one parent and the rest with the other. Some may be currently experiencing their parents' breakup. In this session, they tuned in on the topic with an intense interest and equally intense wariness. Begin by acknowledging these realities and by using the regular practice of reviewing the group agreements.

To give students a way of maintaining some distance from their own experience, provide them with frameworks for understanding divorce (Rollie & Duck, 2006). Explain that sometimes partners are incompatible at the start and that an eventual break-up is inevitable. Other partners grow apart over time and discover that they are unhappy and can no longer be together. A third circumstance occurs when something dramatic happens, like infidelity or betrayal is discovered and the relationship ends abruptly.

Divorces can occur over time and proceed through identifiable stages (Rollie & Duck, 2006). Perhaps one partner feels dissatisfied with the relationship. There may be many possible reasons for this. They may be experiencing depression or other psychological struggle. They may sense a lack of closeness to their partner, resentment from being undervalued, a lack of support, or some other simmering discontent.

Perhaps the partners discuss this dissatisfaction. The other partner may be shocked at the news and have their own problems to air about the relationship. The couple may try to work through this. Sometimes they enter couples therapy. Sometimes issues are resolved. Like the confrontation stage in Sumerlin's relationship model, there may be anger, frustration, guilt, and anxiety experienced as they talk about the problems. Awareness of how other aspects of the relationship enter into the discussion, like their children, family, shared friends, and wider families provokes more difficult conversations.

If resolution doesn't occur, the next stage is when the marital difficulty becomes public. They negotiate about children, assets, and the involvement of the wider network of family and friends. When others know about the difficulties, it becomes difficult to backtrack, deny the problem, and reconcile. It is difficult to avoid blaming each other.

The couple then enters the final stage, when they announce the ending publicly, with each individual providing their own point of view. They may relate different narratives to different people. Support networks become re-established. A post-relationship lifestyle is arranged.

What reactions do you have to this model?
How might understanding this model help others affected by the breakup (children, other family members, and friends)?
What makes a divorce difficult for the partners?
How might a divorce be beneficial to a partner?

How parents resolve their differences through the divorce process and afterward impacts their children and youth. Research found that about half of divorced parents maintain amicable, respectful relationship and seek to cooperate with each other in ways that remain sensitive to the needs of the children (Ahrons, 1994). The other half of parents tends to remain hostile to each other, with animosity and unpleasant interactions characterizing their relationship. Such relationships are distressing to youth, whose needs may be unmet in the quarrelling.

Here are three options to examine the impact of parent separation and divorce on youth, focusing on the youth perspective. One is to write statements or questions on cards and place them face down on a desk in the center of your circle. Go around the circle, with students taking turns selecting a card and responding if they wish, then other students chiming in with their views. Second, use two statements representing diametrically opposite views. Read one statement at a time, asking students to move along an imaginary continuum to indicate their view. Ask them to explain their choice of position. Third, facilitate a large group discussion which is presented here.

Tell the group that some people think that children and youth bear some responsibility for their parents' divorce. Children and youth may sometimes blame themselves for not doing enough to prevent the split, for not being better behaved, for not doing better in school, or for appearing to take one parent's side over the other.

Why do you think children and youth blame themselves for their parents' troubles?

Who really bears the responsibility in the break-up? (Admittedly, this is a leading question, but you can drive home the point that the decisions that adults make about their marriage are theirs alone. Parents are the ones who are responsible for the divorce.)

Youth may feel more protective of one parent and blame one parent more than the other. When is this more likely to occur? (This may be especially true when one parent was unfaithful or betrayed the other. Spousal abuse might be a cause. Local domestic abuse services may provide helpful support groups.)

What feelings might youth have about what happened? (Feelings that youth have about what happened are legitimate and normal. Talking to a trusted adult relative, friend, or counselor may be helpful.)

Parents' divorce requires changes in the lives of the children and youth. What are some of the changes that might occur? (Moving, changing schools, shared custody arrangements may mean living in two households, parents' finances may change affecting what is available to support youth, new routines, reactions of family members, pressures from parents to favor one or the other and increased stress associated with change.)

Use the next three questions as brainstorming processes, listing their ideas on the board.

What can youth ask parents to do to make the divorce and aftermath easier on them? (Avoid putting youth in a position where they feel like they have to take sides. Listen to their children. Pay attention to their children's needs. Communicate about things that affect their children's lives. Be fair about arrangements for living situations, time with the kids, holidays, going to children's activities, and financial support. Be available to kids when they need you. Stay involved in kids' lives. Don't say bad things about the other parent. See a therapist.)

What can youth do for themselves? (Tell parents about their concerns and needs. Communicate when things aren't going well for them. Live their own lives. Take care of themselves physically and emotionally. Avoid using alcohol or other drugs to deal with difficult times and difficult feelings. Make sure you have things to do that are fun. Seek support from others. Talk to a therapist. Talk to siblings. Talk to friend who understands them, like those who also have parents who divorced. Talk to a caring adult relative. Suggest compromises if the parents disagree about something that involves the kids.)

What can relatives, friends, and counselors do for youth whose parents are divorcing? After the divorce happens? (Listen. Offer suggestions. Let them express their feelings. Keep things confidential. Provide opportunities to be away from their parents, like sleepovers. Help them stay positive about themselves.)

Course Closure—Saying Goodbye

Marking the end of the course is an important event. It is a time to reflect on the work you accomplished together, the issues you examined, the discussions you had, the activities you did, and the connections you have made. The last session honors all of these things and more. It is also your disconnection.

Be sure to provide opportunity for each student to have a voice in this ending session and use the designed the activities to allow time for personal, individual reflection followed by sharing with the class. Observe the sharing without interruption.

Course Obituary

Ask students to write their class obituary. You could offer them a template script (Simon et al., 1972) to help them prepare.

(Your name) was a member of (the class). (Pronoun) is remembered for (contribution you made to the class). At the time of (your name)'s departure, (your pronoun) was working on becoming (something you got from the course that you will continue to improve on). (Your pronoun) always wanted, but never got to _____. In lieu of flowers, _____.

A shorter version of a course obituary reads:

Here I sit, about to depart from this course. The class will be remembered for

_____.

See Textbox 12.3 for some responses from a course.

TEXTBOX 12.3. COURSE CLOSURE RESPONSES

- Freedom to be who you are
- Respect of self and others
- Comfort level for all
- Fun
- Openness of opinions
- Acceptance of everyone
- Good discussions
- Honesty
- Supporting each other

Design a Game

This option involves a two-day activity. In the next-to-last class, divide the students into small groups and assign them to design and create a game that their classmates would play on the last day. Ask them to think about the topics, theories, activities, and discussions they had experienced and to then brainstorm board, card, or other types of games. They will design their game using a theme from the course.

They plan how to gather materials and produce their games for the next day's class. None ever missed this assignment. Games they created included their adaptations of destination-type games, like Life and Chutes and Ladders. The latter had spaces on the board where failure to solve problems were marked on the chutes and exhibiting connection behaviors placed them on ladders. Other games included a variety of quiz games where points were earned by answering questions about theories correctly, Relationship Bingo, a version of Monopoly called Monogamy, and many more. Students rotated around the room to play the games. At the end, do a simple closure, where students respond to sentence stems.

At the end of this course I feel . . .
I think . . .
I can say that . . .

Student Choice

Another closure experience involves providing students with a variety of options so they can choose how to express their goodbyes. After explaining the importance of having a closure activity to mark the end of the course, give them some options to consider the day before the last class so that they can prepare for the final day.

TEXTBOX 12.4. EXAMPLES OF COURSE CLOSURE ACTIVITIES

- Write a letter to the class.
- Write a journal entry.
- List the things that felt important to you about the course.
- Draw a symbol or set of symbols.
- Create a mandala.
- Create a graphic image.
- Write a poem.
- Write a song.
- Write a brief skit of students talking about the course.
- Choreograph a dance.
- Just say what comes to mind in class tomorrow.
- Any other form of expression that you can imagine

References

Ahrons, C. (1994). The good divorce. HarperCollins.

Ainsworth, M. D. S., & Bell, S. M. (1970). Attachment, exploration, and separation: Illustrated by the behavior of one-year-olds in a strange situation. *Child Development, 41*, 49–67.

Allport, G. (1954). The nature of prejudice. Addison-Wesley.

Apatow, J. (Director). (2005). The 40-year-old virgin. Universal Pictures.

Attias, D. (Director). (1992). Everybody's talkin' about it [Television series episode]. In A. Spelling (Producer), Beverly Hills 90210. Spelling Television.

Bacev-Giles, C., & Resshma, H. (2017). Online first impressions: Person perception in social media profiles. *Computers in Human Behavior, 75*, 50–57.

Bar, M., Neta, M., & Linz, H. (2006). Very first impressions. *Emotion, 6*, 269–278.

Barrymore, D. (Director). (2009). Whip it [Film]. Fox Searchlight Pictures.

Benitez, C.T., McNiel, D.E., & Binder, R.L. (2010). Do protection orders protect? *Journal of the American Academy of Psychiatry and the Law, 38*(3) 376–385.

Bershad, C., & Blaber, C. (1998). Respecting healthy sexuality. Education Development Center.

Bianchi, S. M., Milkie, M. A., Sayer, L. C., & Robinson, J. P. (2000). Is anyone doing the housework? Trends in the gender division of household labor. *Social Forces, 79*(1), 191–234.

Biello, K.B., Ickovics, J., Niccolai, L., Lin, H., & Kershaw, T. (2013). Racial differences in age at first sexual Intercourse: Residential racial segregation and the black-white disparity among U.S. adolescents. Public Health Reports. 2013 Mar-Apr; 128(Suppl 1): 23–32. doi: 10.1177/00333549131282S103

Bowlby, J. (1958). The nature of the child's tie to his mother. *International Journal of Psychoanalysis, 39*, 350–371.

Bowlby J. (1969). Attachment. Attachment and loss: Vol. 1. Loss. New York: Basic Books.

Boyle, I. (1993). Mighty Pine. In Lusk, J.T. (Ed.), 30 scripts for relaxation imagery and inner healing. Volume 2. Whole Person Associates.

Brotman, J., Casarjian, B., & Casarjian, R. (2005). 30 Scripts for relaxation, imagery & inner healing. Volume 1. Whole Person Associates.

Browning, Elizabeth Barrett, (1906). Sonnets from the Portuguese. Caradoc Press.

Burson, C. (Director). (1999). Coming soon. Lionsgate.

Busseri, M.A.; Willoughby, T., Chalmers, H., & Bogaert, A.R. Same-sex attraction and healthy adolescent development. *Journal of Youth & Adolescence.* Aug 2006, Vol. 35 Issue 4, 561–573. DOI: 10.1007/s10964-006-9071-4.

Buzwell, S., & Rosenthal, D. (1996). Constructing a sexual self: Adolescents' sexual self-perceptions and sexual risk-taking. *Journal of Research on Adolescence, 6*(4), 489–513.

Cacace, R., & Abarca, S. (2016). "You know you want to . . ." In Montfort, S. & Brick, P. (Eds.), *Unequal partners: Teaching about power, consent, and healthy relationships, Volume 1*(3), 111–117. Center for Sex Education.

Carey, B. (2005). The skinny on gossip: Discovering new understandings of gossip and human behavior. New York Times. http://www.nytimes.com/learning/teachers/featured_articles/20050816tuesday.html

Carney, D.R., Colvin, C.R., & Hall, J.A. (2007). A thin slice perspective on the accuracy of first impressions. *Journal of Research in Personality, 41*, 1054–1072.

Carney, J. (Director). (2007). Once [Film]. Summit Entertainment.

Casarjian, B. (2016). The Power source workbook. The LionHeart Foundation.

Casarjian, B., & Casarjian, R. (2003). The Power source facilitators' manual. The LionHeart Foundation.

Castleman, M. (1989). Sexual solutions. Touchstone Books.

Cavert, C. & Frank, L. (Eds.) (1999). Games for teachers: Classroom Activities that promote pro-social learning. Play for Peace.

Centers for Disease Control (2020, August 20). CDC releases youth risk behavior survey results. https://www.cdc.gov/healthyyouth/data/yrbs/feature/index.htm

Chbosky, S. (Director). (2012). Perks of being a wallflower [Film]. Mr. Mudd.

Chudnofsky, R., Johnston, J., & Malloy, L. (n.d.). Learning the relaxation response: Guided meditations for students and adults. Benson-Henry Institute for Mind-Body Medicine.

Cooperman, C. (2014). Sex ed in the digital age (pp. 11–13). The Center for Sex Education.

Cooperman, C., & Rhoades, C. (1982). New methods for puberty education. Planned Parenthood of Northwest New Jersey.

cummings, e.e., (1963). Complete poems. Harcourt Brace Jovanovich.

Darley, J.M., & Gross, P.H. (1983). A hypothesis-confirming bias in labeling effects. *Journal of Personality and Social Psychology, 44*, 20–33.

Dobkin, C. (1999) Toe jam. In Cavert, C. & Frank, L. (Eds.), Games for teachers: Classroom Activities that promote pro-social learning (pp. 121–122). Play for Peace.

Duenwald, M. (2002). Some friends, indeed, do more harm than good. New York Times. https://www.nytimes.com/2002/09/10/health/some-friends-indeed-do-more-harm-than-good.html

Ehrenberg, M., & Ehrenberg, O. (1988). The intimate circle: The sexual dynamics of family life. Simon & Schuster.

Ekman, P. (1970). Universal facial expressions of emotions. *California Mental Health Research Digest, 8*(4), 151–158.

Erikson, E.H. (1963). Childhood and society. Norton.

Erikson, E.H. (1968). Identity: Youth in crisis. Norton.

Fehr, B. (1988). Prototype analysis of the concepts of love and commitment. *Journal of Personality and Social Psychology, 55*(4), 557–579. https://doi.org/10.1037/0022-3514.55.4.557

Fetro, J. (1992). Personal & social skills: Understanding and integrating competencies across health content. ETR.

Frazier, N. & Mehle, D. (2013). Activators: Classroom strategies for engaging middle and high school students. Educators for Social Responsibility.

Furman, W., & Hand, L. S. (2006). The slippery nature of romantic relationships: Issues in definition and differentiation. In A. C. Crouter & A. Booth (Eds.), Romance and sex in adolescence and emerging adulthood: Risks and opportunities (pp. 171–178). Mahwah, NJ: Lawrence Erlbaum Associates.

Gelperin, N. (2013). Activity for "Those cheating hearts: What happens after the betrayal?" SexEtc.org, Sex, Etc. 14. https://sexetc.org/info-center/post/those-cheating-hearts-what-happens-after-the-betrayal/

Gerstein, J. (1999). Classroom poetry. In Cavert, C. & Frank, L. (Eds.), Games for teachers: Classroom Activities that promote pro-social learning (pp. 63–72). Play for Peace.

Giordano, P. C., Manning, W. D., & Longmore, M. A. (2006). Adolescent romantic relationships: An emerging portrait of their nature and developmental significance. In A. C. Crouter & A. Booth (Eds.), Romance and sex in adolescence and emerging adulthood: Risks and opportunities (pp. 127–150). Mahwah, NJ: Lawrence Erlbaum Associates.

Gordon, S. (2021). How to help a teen leave an abusive relationship. https://www.verywellfamily.com/develop-a-safety-plan-for-an-abused-teen-5113941

Goyal, M., Singh, S., Sibinga, E. M.S., Gould, N.F., Rowland-Seymour, A., Sharma, R., Berger, Z., Sleicher, D., Maron, D.D., Shihab, H.M., Ranasinghe, P.D., Linn, S., Saha, S., Bass, E.B., & Haythornthwaite, J.A. (2014). Meditation programs for psychological stress and well-being: A systematic review and meta-analysis. *Journal of the American Medical Association Internal Medicine, 174*(3):357–368.

Hahm, H.C., Lahiff, M. & Barreto, R.M. (2006). Asian American adolescents' first sexual intercourse: Gender and acculturation differences. *Perspectives on Sexual and Reproductive Health, 38*(1):28–36.

Hamric, L. (2019). What can you do when a friendship becomes harmful? [Video]. TED Ed Student Talks.

Hansard, G., & Irglova, M. (2006). Falling slowly [Song recorded by The Swell Season]. The Swell Season. Overcoat Recordings.

Heller, R. (2015). Secular meditation: 32 practices for cultivating inner peace, compassion, and joy. New World Library.

Himelstein, S. (2013) A mindfulness-based approach to working with high-risk adolescents. Routledge.

Hunter-Geboy, C. (2009). Life planning education: A youth development program. Advocates for Youth.

InteraXon, Inc. (2021). EEG-powered sleep tracking and meditation. https://choosemuse.com/

Jackson E., Galvin J., Warrier V., Baron-Cohen, S., Luo, S., Dunbar, R., Proctor, H., Lee, E., & Richards, G. (2002). Evidence of assortative mating for theory of mind via facial expressions but not language. *Journal of Social & Personal Relationships, 39*(12):3660–3679. doi:10.1177/02654075221106451.

Jandernoa, E. (September, 1973). Hall counselor training. Indiana University of Pennsylvania.

Javidi, H., Maheux, A.J., Widman, L., Kamke, K., Choukas-Bradley, S., & Peterson, Z.D. (2020). Understanding adolescents' attitudes toward affirmative consent. *Journal of Sex Research, 57*(9), 1100–1107. doi: 10.1080/00224499.2019.1711009.

Jean, B.C., & Gad, T. (2008). If I were a boy [Recorded by Beyoncé Knowles]. On I Am . . . Sasha Fierce. Columbia Records.

Kabat-Zinn, J. (1994). Wherever you go, there you are: Mindfulness meditation in everyday life. Hyperion Books.

Kabat-Zinn, J. (2012). Mindfulness for beginners: Reclaiming the present moment—and your life. Sounds True, Inc.

Kagan, J. (2007). What is Emotion? Yale University Press.

Kilner, C. (Director). (2009). American virgin [Film]. Echo Bridge Entertainment.

Kirby, D. (2000). What does the research say about sexuality education? *Educational Leadership, 58*, 72–76.

Kvarnstrom, J., & Schramm, S. (1989). Beneath the waves: Sounds of the humpback whales and music. NorthSound.

Kwapis, K. (Director). (2005). The sisterhood of the traveling pants. Warner Brothers.

Lee, J.A. (1988). Love-styles. In R. Sternberg & M. Barnes (Eds.), The psychology of love. Yale University Press.

Lehmiller, J.J. (2009). Secret romantic relationships: Consequences for personal and relational well-being. *Personality and Social Psychology Bulletin, 35*(11), 1452–1466.

Levitin, D.J. (2006). This is your brain on music. Plume.

Logan, T.K., & Walker, R. (2011). Civil protective orders effective in stopping or reducing partner violence. Policy Brief No. 18, Carsey Institute.

Lowenstein, T. (2015, November 11). Biodots: Small circles test your stress by measuring hand temperature. Stress, Anxiety, Biofeedback, Relaxation Skills. http://stressmarket.blogspot.com/2015/12/biodots-small-circles-test-your-stress.html

Luft, J. and Ingham, H. (1955) "The Johari window, a graphic model of interpersonal awareness," Proceedings of the western training laboratory in group development. Los Angeles: UCLA.

Lusk, J. (1992). 30 scripts for relaxation imagery and inner healing. Volume 1. Whole Person Associates.

Lusk, J. (1993). 30 scripts for relaxation imagery and inner healing. Volume 2. Whole Person Associates.

Marchetta, E. (2013). Those cheating hearts: What happens after the betrayal? SexEtc.org, Sex, Etc. 14. https://sexetc.org/info-center/post/those-cheating-hearts-what-happens-after-the-betrayal/

Marcus, D.K., & Miller, R.R. (2003). Sex differences in judgements of physical attractiveness: A social relations analysis. *Personality and Social Psychology Bulletin, 29*, 325–335.

Mark, K., Janssen, E., & Milhausen, R. (2011). Infidelity in heterosexual couples: Demographic, interpersonal, and personality-related predictors of extradyadic sex. Archives of Sexual Behavior. doi:10.1007/s10508-011-977-z

Marshall, P. (Director). (2001). Riding in cars with boys [Film]. Columbia Pictures.

Martin, K. (1996). Puberty, sexuality, and the self. Routledge and Kegan Paul.

Masterson, M.S. (Director). (2007) The cake eaters [Film]. Screen Media Films.

Mayer, J.D., & Salovey, P. (1997). What is emotional intelligence? In P. Salovey & D. Schuyter (Eds.), Emotional development and emotional intelligence: Educational implications (pp. 3–34). Basic Books.

Mayo Clinic Staff. (2011). Being assertive: Reduce stress, communicate better. Mayo Foundation for Medical Education and Research (MFMER). http://www.mayoclinic.com/health/assertive/SR00042

McAndrew, F.T. (2008). The psychology of gossip. (pp. 5–7). Psychology Teacher Network.

Meyers, L. (2007). The eternal question: Does love last? *Monitor on Psychology.* https://www.apa.org/monitor/feb07/eternal

Miller, R.S., & Perlman, D. (2009). Intimate relationships. McGraw Hill.

Moles, K. (2001). The teen relationship workbook: For professionals helping teens to develop healthy relationships and prevent domestic violence. Wellness Reproductions & Publishing.

Musick, J. (2008). Instructor's manual for Crooks and Baur's our sexuality (10th ed.). Thomson Wadsworth.

Obear, K. (1981). Opening doors to understanding and acceptance: A facilitator's guide to presenting workshops on lesbian and gay issues. The Human Advantage.

Oliver, J. (1992). Music for relaxation. The Relaxation Company.

Parker, O. (Director). (2005). Imagine me & you [Film]. Twentieth Century Fox.

Perez, E. (2017). The state of affairs: Rethinking infidelity. Harper.

Planned Parenthood Federation of America. (2022). Sexual consent. https://www.plannedparenthood.org/learn/relationships/sexual-consent

Pollmann, M.M.H., & Finkenauer, C. (2009). Investigating the role of two types of understanding in relationship well-being: Understanding is more important than knowledge. *Personality and Social Psychology Bulletin, 35*, 1512–1527.

Prince-Bythewood, G. (Director). (2000). Love & basketball [Film]. New Line Cinema.

Redford, R. (Director). (1980). Ordinary people [Film]. Paramount Pictures.

Rhoades, C. (2007). Ethical considerations in the use of sexually explicit visuals as an instructional methodology in college sexuality courses. *American Journal of Sexuality Education, 2*(4), 5–23.

Rhoades, C., & Bradeen-Knox, C. (1992). Listen to the students: A student-centered curriculum for HIV/AIDS education and prevention. Family Planning Association of Maine.

Rhoades, C., Pierce-Glover, J., & Ruchinskas, M. (2017). Pilot-Testing a psycho-educational group program with homeless youth. Presentation at the American Psychological Association annual conference. Washington, D.C.

Rollie, S.S., & Duck, S. (2006). Divorce and dissolution of romantic relationships: Stage models and their limitations. In M.A. Fine & J.H. Harvey (Eds.), Handbook of divorce and relationship dissolution (pp. 223–240), Erlbaum.

Rubin, Z. (1970). Measurement of romantic love. *Journal of Personality and Social Psychology, 16*, 265–273.

Schwartz, A.E. (1995). Guided imagery for groups. Whole Person Associates.

Sharpsteen, D. J., & Kirkpatrick, L. A. (1997). Romantic jealousy and adult romantic attachment. *Journal of Personality and Social Psychology, 72*(3), 627–640. https://doi.org/10.1037/0022-3514.72.3.627

Simon, S.S., Howe, L.W., & Kirschenbaum, H. (1972). Values clarification: A handbook of practical strategies for teachers and students. Hart-Publishing.

Skeen, M., McKay, M., Fanning, P., & Skeen, K. (2016). Communication skills for teens. New Harbringer Publications.

Solomon, A.H. (2019). Do you believe in soul mates? Should you? Psychology Today. https://www.psychologytoday.com/us/blog/loving-bravely/201901/do-you-believe-in-soulmates-should-you

Soto, G. (2009). Partly cloudy: Poems of love and longing. Harcourt.

Sternberg, R.J. (1988). The triangle of love. New York: Basic Books.

Stiller, B. (Director). (1994). Reality bites [Film]. Jersey Films.

Stinson, D.A., Cameron, J.J., Hoplock, L.B. (2021). The friends-to-lovers pathway to romance: Prevalent, preferred, and overlooked by science. *Social Psychological and Personality Science*. doi:10.1177/19485506211026992.

Sumerlin, J.R. (1979). Development of exclusive romantic primary pair bonds: Construct validation of a five stage theory. Publication No. 8010307. [Doctoral Dissertation, New York University]. ProQuest Dissertations & Theses Global.

Sumner, W.G. (1906). Folkways: A study of the sociological importance of usages, manners, customs, mores, and morals. Ginn.

Sunnafrank, M., & Ramirez, A., Jr. (2004). At first sight: Persistent relational effects of get-acquainted conversations. *Journal of Social and Personal Relationships, 21*, 361–379.

TEDx, (2013, May 22). The sexual experience: Let's talk about it / Orit Mordekovitch [Video]. YouTube. https://m.youtube.com/watch?v=LrG3EDY3UV8

Thompson, C. (1987). Mutual caring, mutual sharing: A sexuality education unit for adolescents. Strafford County Prenatal & Family Planning Program (The Clinic).

Tolman, D.L. (2002). Dilemmas of desire. Harvard University Press.

Truth, L. (2007). Anniversary. *The Sun.* https://www.thesunmagazine.org/issues/378/anniversary

Vance, C. (1984). Pleasure and danger: Toward a politics of sexuality. In C.S. Vance (ed.), Pleasure and danger: Exploring female sexuality. Routledge and Kegan Paul.

Varia, S. (2006). Dating violence among adolescents. Advocates for Youth.

Weiss, R.S. (1973). Loneliness. MIT Press.

Williams, W.C. (1986). XXII: The red wheelbarrow. In Litz & MacGowan (Eds.) The collected poems of William Carlos Williams, I: 1909–1939. New Directions Books.

Willis, J., & Todorov, A. (2006). First impressions: Making up your mind after a 100-ms exposure to a face. *Psychological Science, 17*, 131–134.

Winter, P. (1997). Canyon Lullaby. Earth Music Productions.

Yates, P. (Director and Producer). (1979). Breaking away [Film]. Twentieth Century Fox.

Zemeckis, R. (1994). Forrest Gump [Film]. Paramount.

Zilbergeld, B. (1991). The new male sexuality. Bantom.

Zillmann, D. (1984). Connections between sex and aggression. Hillsdale, NJ: Erlbaum.

Index

passive communication, 101–2. *See also* communication

Perks of Being a Wallflower, 81

permission, *See* consent

poetry, 14–15. poems about relationships, 30–31

Power Source, 2, 19, 45–46, 49, 68, 79, 110, 166

problem-solving steps, 117–22

problems, 2, 45–46, 49, 68, 79, *115–35*, 166

pronouns, 2–3, 73

Reality Bites, 80–81

reciprocity, 89, 91

relatives, 35, 51, 168. *See also* family

Riding in Cars with Boys, 68–69

Rubin, Zick, 72–73

secrecy, 92

self-discovery, 17–18, 137

sexual behavior, 122, 137–38, 145, 148–49. *See also* consent; first sexual experiences; infidelity; touch continuum

sexual communication styles, 145–46

sexual orientation, 33, 57, 69, 88, 123, 138, 158. *See also* LGBTQ+

Sexuality Attitude Reassessment Training, 137–38

sexually healthy relationship, 154–55

Sisterhood of the Travelling Pants, 52

social isolation, 53

songs about relationships, 29–30

soul mates, 68

stages of relationships, 78–80, 146

starting a relationship, 83–92

Sternberg, Robert, 74–75, 81, 146

substance use, 47, 78–81, 84, 152

Sumerlin, John, 146

texting, 48, 87–89, 108, 160, 162

touch continuum, 142–45, 148, 151

transgender, 2, 138. *See also* gender; LGBTQ+

trauma, 19, 21, 81, 115, 117

Triangular Theory of Love, 74–75

values, 44, 59–65, 126, 138, 154

violence, 33, 45, 61, 64, 158. *See also* abuse

Whip it, 51–52

Zillmann, Dolph, 75–76